SECOND-DEGREE
BLACK BELT
SUDOKU®

Frank Longo

**PUZZLE
WRIGHT
PRESS**

An imprint of Sterling
Publishing Co., Inc.
www.puzzlewright.com

CONTENTS

12

Published by Sterling Publishing Co., Inc.
387 Park Avenue South, New York, NY 10016
© 2005 by Sterling Publishing Co., Inc.
Distributed in Canada by Sterling Publishing
C/o Canadian Manda Group, 165 Dufferin Street
Toronto, Ontario, Canada M6K 3H6
Distributed in the United Kingdom by GMC Distribution Services
Castle Place, 166 High Street, Lewes, East Sussex, England BN7 1XU
Distributed in Australia by Capricorn Link (Australia) Pty. Ltd.
P.O. Box 704, Windsor, NSW 2756, Australia

Manufactured in Canada

Sterling ISBN 978-1-4027-3717-6

For information about custom editions, special sales, premium and corporate purchases, please contact Sterling Special Sales Department at 800-805-5489 or specialsales@sterlingpublishing.com.

INTRODUCTION

To solve sudoku puzzles, all you need to know is this one simple rule:

Fill in the boxes so that the nine rows, the nine columns, and the nine 3×3 sections all contain every digit from 1 to 9.

And that's all there is to it! Using this simple rule, let's see how far we get on this sample puzzle at right. (The letters at the top and left edges of the puzzle are for reference only; you won't see them in the regular puzzles.)

	A	B	C	D	E	F	G	H	I
J									
K					2		1	8	4
L	9		5		7		2		6
M	1		4	3	9	2		7	
N				7		6			
O		7		1	4	8	9		2
P	3		2		6		8		5
Q	8	4	9		3				
R									

The first number that can be filled in is an obvious one: box EN is the only blank box in the center 3×3 section, and all the digits 1 through 9 are represented except for 5. EN must be 5.

The next box is a little trickier to discover. Consider the upper left 3×3 section of the puzzle. Where can a 4 go? It can't go in AK, BK, or CK because row K already has a 4 at IK. It can't go in BJ or BL because column B already has a 4 at BQ. It can't go in CJ because column C already has a 4 at CM. So it must go in AJ.

Another box in that same section that can now be filled is BJ. A 2 can't go in AK, BK, or CK due to the 2 at EK. The 2 at GL rules out a 2 at BL. And the 2 at CP means that a 2 can't go in CJ. So BJ must contain the 2. It is worth noting that this 2 couldn't have been placed without the 4 at AJ in place.

Many of the puzzles rely on this type of steppingstone behavior.

We now have a grid as shown.

Let's examine column A. There are four blank boxes in column A; in which blank box must the 2 be placed? It can't be AK because of the 2 in EK (and the 2 in BJ). It can't be AO because of the 2 in IO. It can't be AR because of the 2 in CP. Thus, it must be AN that has the 2.

	A	B	C	D	E	F	G	H	I
J	4	2							
K					2		1	8	4
L	9		5		7		2		6
M	1		4	3	9	2		7	
N				7	5	6			
O		7		1	4	8	9		2
P	3		2		6		8		5
Q	8	4	9		3				
R									

3

By the 9's in AL, EM, and CQ, box BN must be 9. Do you see how?

We can now determine the value for box IM. Looking at row M and then column I, we find all the digits 1 through 9 are represented but 8. IM must be 8.

This brief example of some of the techniques leaves us with the grid at right.

You should now be able to use what you learned to fill in CN followed by BL, then HL followed by DL and FL.

As you keep going through this puzzle, you'll find it gets easier as you fill in more. And as you keep working through the puzzles in this book, you'll find it gets easier and more fun each time. The final answer is shown below.

	A	B	C	D	E	F	G	H	I
J	4	2							
K					2		1	8	4
L	9		5		7		2		6
M	1		4	3	9	2		7	8
N	2	9		7	5	6			
O		7		1	4	8	9		2
P	3		2		6		8		5
Q	8	4	9		3				
R									

This book consists of 300 puzzles of super-tough level of difficulty.

—Frank Longo

	A	B	C	D	E	F	G	H	I
J	4	2	1	6	8	3	5	9	7
K	7	3	6	5	2	9	1	8	4
L	9	8	5	4	7	1	2	3	6
M	1	5	4	3	9	2	6	7	8
N	2	9	8	7	5	6	4	1	3
O	6	7	3	1	4	8	9	5	2
P	3	1	2	9	6	7	8	4	5
Q	8	4	9	2	3	5	7	6	1
R	5	6	7	8	1	4	3	2	9

1

	1	8			4			
				8				3
3	9		5				4	
			6		7	2	3	9
6	4	2	9		1			
	8				9		2	4
4				6				
			4			7	8	

2

		7			9		8	
						7		3
		4	8	3			2	
	5		4			9		
	1						4	
		9			6		1	
	7			2	3	4		
8		6						
	2		5			6		

3

	2			6				9
8			2			5		
					8	6		
9		5	7					2
		6		8		4		
2				5		9		6
		1	7					
		7			3			4
4				9			1	

4

				1				4
			8		2		3	
		7			4	5		
	4			5		8		2
7								9
8		9		3			6	
		6	5			1		
	5			2		6		
4				9				

5

		9				6		
	2		8	3			1	
							9	8
			1		7			9
1								3
7			5		3			
8	5							
	7			2	6		4	
		3				7		

6

		1	7					
	4	3		1	9			
		5					6	8
				7			4	
	7	9	4		5	8	3	
	6			3				
4	3					6		
			5	9		3	8	
					3	7		

7

	8	4			2		6	
		1	7	6				
		9		8				1
		7	8			6		
	4						1	
		8			1	2		
2				3		1		
				7	8	5		
	9		1			7	2	

8

3					5			9
	9						2	
		4		8			7	
				2	7	9	1	
		9		1		4		
	1	8	5	4				
	4			5		8		
	2						9	
8			6					2

9

2			4			9		
		5		1				
					5	4	3	2
				2			6	7
	6			3			8	
1	7			9				
7	2	9	8					
				4		7		
		4			1			3

10

			2			9	6	
8			7		3	2		
					9		4	
1						5		
		2		9		3		
		7						2
	9		4					
		1	5		2			6
	7	8			1			

Puzzle 1/1

				4	2	3	6	
	7					2	1	
			7					
6			9				5	2
				5				
7	1				6			4
					8			
	3	9					2	
	4	8	2	3				

Puzzle 1/2

			1	5		6	9	
		8		3				
2					4	7		
6						9	2	
5								7
	8	4						6
		9	6					1
				8		3		
	1	5		4	3			

Puzzle 1/3

		2			3	7		
					5	1		3
		9					4	
4				7			2	
	3			9			1	
	2			3				5
	4					8		
2		6	1					
		8	3			5		

Puzzle 1/4

	9			4			3	
		7	8			4	1	
					6			
	1	8	5	3			9	
	3			1	7	8	2	
			4					
	7	6			9	1		
	4			2			5	

Puzzle 1/5

			9			2		1
		9			1		8	
						3	7	
		7		6			3	
	4			2			5	
	6			1		8		
	7	6						
	2		3			9		
5		1			4			

Puzzle 1/6

4					7	3		
		3						
	8		4		1			
	1						4	6
	6	4		1		8	5	
7	9						2	
			6		5		7	
						4		
		9	8					1

17

	8						1	
5		7			4	9		
					3			5
1					5			6
	7		9		8		4	
4			6					7
6			3					
		2	8			6		4
	1						2	

18

5					8	4	9	7
					7			
3		8		4				
	5	7			6		4	
		2	4		9	5		
	9		7			3	2	
				7		1		4
			6					
7	4	5	8					2

Puzzle 19

	2	6	5					
			3				4	
5					6	2		3
		3			8		6	
		7		9		4		
	6		4			3		
8		9	2					6
	5				7			
					5	7	8	

Puzzle 20

							7	5
		6	3		7			9
3	5			1				
						9	5	
9		1				6		4
	4	5						
				2			4	7
5			8		3	2		
6	2							

14

		4					2	8
		8	2	6		9		
9	2		3					1
	4		5				1	
				8				
	7				2		3	
3					7		8	6
		7		2	3	4		
4	9					2		

4			3		7			
						4	9	3
		6		5				
		1		8				6
3		7	9		5	2		8
8				1		5		
				2		3		
6	5	3						
			6		9			4

Puzzle 2/3

	9						8	1
	7		8	5				2
					6	5		
5				1	3	7		
		1	7	4				6
		9	4					
7				2	9		1	
2	3						4	

Puzzle 2/4

5					9		8	
			6					7
4				2			1	
					7		5	3
7	9						6	8
6	5		9					
	2			3				1
8					6			
	1		2					9

5

				7				
9	7		1					
4	5	1	9				7	
5		7			3	1	2	
	1	2	7			4		9
	6				9	5	1	8
					6		4	7
			8					

26

		6			5			3
8					1		2	
				9		6		
		7	1			5		8
		4				9		
1		5			7	2		
		9		3				
	3		7					9
5			6			3		

		5	8			6	4	
	9	4			1			
			4	3				
	5	6			3		8	
				1				
	3		5			9	1	
				4	8			
			6			4	7	
	6	2			7	1		

7			9	8				5
					2			3
		6		7				
	1			3		5		4
	4						3	
3		9		2			1	
				4		2		
8			1					
5				6	9			8

29

					3			
	8				1		3	
	5		8	2		6		9
4						3	9	
6		7		4		5		8
	9	3						4
1		9		7	8		6	
	7		1				8	
			5					

30

		4	9		7			
							3	
8		6	3			7		
6				2				
	5		6		3		7	
				5				9
		1			6	5		2
	6							
			2		5	8		

Puzzle 3/1:

4		7				2		
5	2							9
			4					8
			8				6	
	8		7	3	9		5	
	5				6			
8					3			
9							7	4
		6				9		3

Puzzle 3/2:

	9		7					
	7						1	5
4		5		2				
		8			9	6		
5		2		7		9		4
		9	8			5		
				5		3		9
9	8						5	
					6		4	

Puzzle 3/3

5								9
6	1	7		2				
	3					1	6	
1		9			5			
			8	7	6			
			4			3		8
	9	1					8	
				8		4	1	2
8								5

Puzzle 3/4

7						8	4	
	6				5			
4			1				6	
9					7	4		
		8				9		
		4	9					5
	1				6			2
			7				1	
	4	2						8

3/5

		2	6	8				
	9				3	2	8	
	7							5
		4			1			
1			2		4			6
			7			4		
9							7	
	8	6	3				5	
				2	8	3		

3/6

		3		8	7	6		1
1		4					2	
7			3		8			
8				1				3
			9		5			7
	8					2		6
5		9	2	3		1		

3/7

5	3							
	8							9
4		9	7	5				1
	5		6		8			
		8		9		2		
			4		5		6	
3				4	6	8		2
1							4	
							3	7

3/8

					4			
	4			1	8	2		
1		6					4	
		9			2	8		5
				6				
3		1	4			9		
	8					7		2
		7	8	2			1	
			9					

Puzzle 39

		4	8		6			
		9	2	1				
3								1
						9		8
	6		4	2	8		3	
2		5						
4								6
				6	7	2		
			1		4	8		

Puzzle 40

		1						
		2	4		9		7	
		5				2		1
	5	7		3				
			2	7	8			
			5			3	8	
2		8				7		
	4		7		3	6		
						1		

4 1

6	5			9			8	3
	9	1			8			
							2	
			4			5		1
				6				
7		4			9			
	3							
			7			8	1	
1	6			4			7	2

4 2

	9		8			5		
						3		4
	2			5			9	
2	1		5					6
			6		3			
6					1		7	8
	4			9			8	
5		1						
		8			5	4		

4 3

	6		3			9	4	
					4		5	3
					6			2
	7				1	3		
	3						7	
		5	6				1	
3			8					
8	4		5					
	1	2			7		6	

4 4

			8			7		1
5				9			8	
				2		4		
1	5						2	
	3		5		1		7	
	4						1	8
		8		1				
	2			7				6
3		7			4			

		4					6	
		9		4				
1			9	5			4	
5		2	8				1	
	4						8	
	9				3	6		5
	1			3	2			8
				7		3		
	3					1		

							1	
4		5		9			7	
	6	3	8					
			3					1
9		1		8		6		5
8					9			
					8	4	2	
	5			3		1		8
	2							

					9			1
		6	3		4			
				7		9	2	
						3		9
	8	5		4		6	1	
7		3						
	5	4		2				
			4		7	2		
3			1					

		2						
8		9				5	4	
			9	8			6	
		7			6	4		
	4		5		3		2	
		6	2			9		
	2			4	7			
	3	4				7		2
						3		

2		6			5	4		
				6			3	
	9	1						5
		8	7	9			5	
				5				
	2			1	3	9		
3						6	2	
	4			3				
		2	6			1		3

			2	9		1		3
	8						4	
		9	1					
	2		5					4
	4	1		3		7	6	
6					9		1	
					8	4		
	7						9	
5		4		6	1			

5-1

								3
	2		1				5	
6	3	1			8			
3			8	2		5		
	8		3		5		6	
		9		6	1			7
			2			7	4	5
	4				6		8	
1								

5-2

	6				8			
	2	5					6	
			1	2				5
	4			8				2
			7		2			
1				9			3	
9				3	7			
	7					4	8	
			6				9	

Puzzle 5-3

	7				5			
		4		1				
6				7		5		9
					3	8		7
9		3				2		1
7		1	6					
1		2	9					4
			5			1		
			7				2	

Puzzle 5-4

5		1						9
					3	7		4
	3				4		8	1
		6	5		2		4	
	1		7		6	8		
6	5		8				7	
1		2	3					
4						1		8

Puzzle 5 5

6	5			2			4	
			7	3	9	8		
						3		
9					5	2	6	
	2	6	9					4
		4						
		8	6	7	3			
	6			1			9	3

Puzzle 5 6

	9							1
		7			8	6		
			7				9	
			9	6				5
5	1						4	2
4				5	1			
	2				5			
		1	8			3		
3							2	

Puzzle 5/7

		7	5	6	3			
						9		
	3			4			8	6
4		1	7					
	8						7	
					5	8		4
6	5			7			9	
		4						
			6	3	8	4		

Puzzle 5/8

			2	4				
1		5					8	
		8			5		9	
9							6	
		3	6		4	5		
	2							9
	3		4			7		
	7					9		6
				2	9			

				5			3	
8		6	1		9			
			8				9	
		3				6		4
			3	1	2			
9		7				1		
	5				1			
			7		4	9		5
	4			2				

5		1					8	
		8	1		9			
	9	2		8				
			9	3				6
	4						7	
9				5	7			
				6		5	3	
			3		1	2		
	3					8		4

6-1

		2			5			
3	5					7		
9			6		2			
		7		4		8	5	
		9				3		
	1	4		3		6		
			1		3			6
		5					7	3
			2			9		

6-2

		7	1	4			3	6
	4		7		6		1	
		6						7
5								
			3	8	1			
								2
9						3		
	1		2		7		9	
3	8			1	9	7		

6 / 3

					3			
			8	5		4	9	
5		2		6				8
		5			7		6	1
2								4
1	9		6			8		
8				4		7		5
	5	6		8	9			
			3					

6 / 4

6		1		8				
			1		4			
	8			2				7
	1	2					6	
8		6	4		1	7		9
	7					5	8	
9				4			1	
			8		3			
				1		8		5

Puzzle 6/5

	7			4	5		3	
					3	6		5
8			2					
		4	5			7		
		1				2		
		6			9	4		
					8			4
3		5	6					
	6		9	5			1	

Puzzle 6/6

			6	8	4		2	1
		2						
					5		3	8
		7					5	
5			7		9			3
	1					4		
6	7		5					
						1		
2	3		9	6	8			

Puzzle 67:

		7			9			
2						1	4	
9	6		3					
					4		5	8
				8				
3	1		2					
					8		3	2
	8	9						6
			9			8		

Puzzle 68:

1				2			4	
5	9		3			7		
					4		6	
	4				7			6
		2				5		
6			8				9	
	5		6					
		8			5		7	1
	7			4				9

Puzzle 69

9				6	1			3
	5	7			4			
		1						2
	1							7
		3		9		6		
5							8	
1						8		
			8			3	2	
7			5	2				1

Puzzle 70

			1				2	
		4	9				6	7
5				6	4	1		
			4					
	4	6		1		3	5	
					5			
		7	6	3				9
8	3				9	6		
	9				8			

Puzzle 7/1:

					8		4	
1			6	3				
3			5				8	
	6					4		
4			9	6	3			5
		9					2	
	7				5			2
				9	2			7
	2		3					

Puzzle 7/2:

7	6						8	
8	2				4			3
				5			6	
6					1			7
			4	8	6			
3			7					4
	1			4				
2			9				4	8
	7						3	2

Puzzle 7/3

4				6	9			
	3		8					
	6	2						5
1	9			7		6		
		6		2		7		
		7		4			9	1
5						1	3	
					7		2	
			5	8				7

Puzzle 7/4

		6	8					3
		1	7	2		9		
4			6					
	4						3	
2			1	3	5			6
	6						1	
					7			2
		8		6	2	5		
9				1		6		

75

	4					3	6	
	1		9		2			7
		2						
5		4		7		1		
			5		9			
		8		6		7		3
						8		
1			3		5		2	
	6	3					7	

76

				4			1	2
4				7				
	7		3				5	4
	8		9				7	
		5		8		6		
	6				3		2	
1	5				9		8	
				3				7
8	9			5				

7 / 7

	9				3			
1			7				2	
6	3				2			
5	6	7				4		
		8				7	9	5
			8				5	2
	7				1			3
			3				4	

7 / 8

3	6		8					7
	4					6		1
	9		6					
		7	4		8			3
				5				
8			2		3	4		
					5		1	
6		2					5	
1					2		8	6

79

		4			8		1	
	8		9	7				
				3		9		8
8						5		
5	3			6			8	7
		7						2
2		6	1					
			5	4			3	
	4		8			7		

80

	2				4	8	5	
		8						
			6	9				3
	3					5	2	
5			9		2			1
	7	1					6	
1				8	9			
						4		
	6	2	5				1	

Puzzle 8/1

						6		
	3		4					5
		2	3	5		7		
7	8		5		1		3	
				4				
	5		2		8		7	9
		6		7	5	3		
3					9		4	
		1						

Puzzle 8/2

	7	3	2		9			
4	8						9	
	6			7				
3				1	2			5
8			7	4				2
				2			7	
	4						3	1
			9		1	4	6	

			1				4	
	2	3						8
5			6			1	2	
	4		3			5	6	
			4		6			
	6	5			9		1	
	9	8			2			1
3						2	8	
	1				3			

								7
	1					8		9
			9	3		6		
	3				2	4		
			7	8	4			
		2	5				8	
		3		6	1			
2		8					3	
5								

8/5

6		4		5				
	9				8			
				3		2	9	
1	8			7				2
	7		4		6		8	
9				2			7	5
	1	9		6				
			5				2	
				8		4		7

8/6

			7					
	4			5	1		6	
			6			4		9
							1	3
	7	3				2	9	
4	8							
9		2			6			
	6		2	8			5	
					7			

Puzzle 8/7

6		3					7	
					8			
4	1		2					
7			8	5		4		
9								6
		4		7	3			2
					2		6	1
			5					
	7					8		3

Puzzle 8/8

1		6		7				
2			9					7
4	9	7			1			
		4				5		2
			5		4			
8		1				9		
			1			2	8	5
5					2			1
				9		3		4

		8						
	3			2	4	1		7
	7	9		5				2
3	4				8		7	
	8		9				6	4
7				3		4	2	
2		4	1	8			3	
						9		

		9		6			7	
			4	1	2			
	2					6		1
	3	6			4	5		
		4	1			7	3	
9		3					8	
			3	2	1			
	5			9		4		

9/1

		5	7			2	6	
					8	4		
	7				2			8
5		9	2					4
7			3					1
8			7			3		6
1			4				8	
		8	2					
	9	3				7	6	

9/2

						8	3	1
					1			
	2	4		5	3			6
	7		5			4		
			3	8	7			
		5			4		9	
3			7	9		6	2	
			1					
5	4	6						

Puzzle 9-3

		3			7		4	8
				6		1	2	
8								3
	9		8		6		1	
				4				
	4		1		2		3	
3								4
	1	6		8				
2	7		6			5		

Puzzle 9-4

			2					
		2			8	1	7	
6		4	9					5
2		5				4		
	1						3	
		3				5		6
8					2	3		4
	3	9	4			8		
					3			

1		9		3		4		
				4		5		
	2		8				6	3
	4	1	6					9
				2				
2					3	7	4	
4	3				9		7	
		2		8				
		8		7		2		4

2				1	7			
8						4	9	
9					8	2		
			4			6		
	2			5			8	
		5			1			
		4	3					7
	3	2						8
			1	9				4

				6		4	5	8
9					4		7	
			7		3			
	9	2				6	3	
	1	3				7	4	
			3		6			
	7		5					1
4	5	8		2				

	1				2	7	8	
					3			
	6			4				5
6						5		
	9	2		1		6	3	
		5						4
7				8			5	
			9					
	3	9	6				2	

5					8	2		
8		6					5	
	2			3				
9	5	7	2				6	
6								1
	1				4	5	9	7
				5			1	
	4					6		5
		5	6					4

	1				3	8		
			5		6			
	2	6				7	5	
6		2						1
	3	7	8		9	4	2	
9						3		7
	5	8				2	7	
			4		7			
		3	2				4	

101

4					5	8		
				7				
6	2	3	4					
	6		7			3		8
3	4			5			6	7
5		7			6		4	
					9	5	2	4
				4				
		4	8					9

102

			1		4			7
	9				7	1	4	
			3					2
		8		3			9	
	2			6		4		
7					1			
	4	1	9				8	
6			5		2			

					6		9	
	2	6	9			3		
	7	1			4			
5								8
			5	6	3			
7								1
			3			7	5	
		7			9	1	2	
	4		7					

			6	2	1			4
	3	6	4			1		7
3	1						9	
		8				5		
	5						7	1
1		7			3	9	8	
4			1	9	6			

105

	6		8				5	
9		4				6		
	7	8		5			9	
		2	1	6				
				9	2	7		
	2			7		4	6	
		1				8		9
	8				6		2	

106

3			4			1		
			7			5		8
	2		3	5			7	4
	8				4	2		
7								3
		4	5				8	
6	3			1	5		4	
5		1			6			
		8			7			1

				6	5		2	7
2					4			
		5	2			8	6	
6						7	4	
		2				6		
	8	7						5
	7	3			9	2		
			7					1
9	5		1	3				

2		3		6			1	
	7		2	5				
9						1	2	
		5	3					2
			5		7			
4					8	5		
		8	9					5
				7	2		3	
	9			3		1		4

		7						
		5	7	3	6			
	8	6					7	4
2	7		3	6				
		1				8		
			7	1			9	2
8	6					2	3	
			9	8	2	7		
						4		

1	2		6		4			
		5				2		3
8	3							
2		4	7		6			
			9		2	6		5
							8	1
9		6				7		
			8		5		6	2

6				7	8			9
		2		4			5	
			6			7		2
	6	7						3
4								5
9						8	1	
2		3			4			
	4			9		5		
5			1	3				4

6						4	3	
2	7	4				9		
				9				
4			1		6			
5			7		4			3
			9		8			7
				8				
		5				1	7	8
	1	6						4

113

		2			7		1	8
						2		
	3				1		6	9
	6		4	9		5	7	
	9	5		7	6		3	
6	8		5				2	
		1						
5	7		6			1		

114

							9	
6		7						8
		3			5		7	
			7		1		5	6
9				5				3
4	5		3		2			
	2		9			4		
1						8		5
	8							

		6	9				3	
								6
8	5				7			1
	1				4	7		9
			1		3			
2		9	8				1	
1			2				9	4
6								
	4					1	3	

	3		6					
	2				8	3		
	6		1	4				
8	1							
		4				9		
							3	2
				6	7		5	
		5	8				4	
					9		6	

8	3		6				7	
	4					9	3	
					9	6		
7			5		2	1		9
				3				
4		2	9		8			7
		8	4					
	1	4					9	
	5				3		4	6

	6	1	8			5		
				4				
2					3		6	7
5		6				9		4
	7						5	
1		4				7		6
9	8		4					2
				3				
		5			1	4	7	

	7	8	4					
5						8		9
3		6		2				
		5					9	2
	2		5		6		7	
8	1					5		
				8		9		7
7		9						5
					4	2	8	

8					4	7		2
4			5					3
							1	
	5			7		2		
	4		6		9		3	
		6		4			7	
	1							
6					3			8
7		9	1					6

Puzzle 121

6	7					8	3	
				4		6		
	5				3			4
3	1			7				
		8				3		
				8			9	1
1			9				2	
		3		1				
	2	7					5	8

Puzzle 122

	7	8			3	5		6
								3
3				5	6	4		
4					5			
		2		7		9		
			2					1
		3	9	4				8
6								
9		4	3			7	1	

		3	4		9	2		
	6			8	2			7
2								
		5			8			
4		2		1		7		8
			9			4		
								3
1			7	2			6	
		7	8		4	9		

		4					8	
			1		5			3
		7		4				
		1			6		3	
	9		2		8		1	
	6		9			7		
				2		9		
5			7		1			
	1					8		

125

	4				2	8		
				9		4	7	5
	7		8				1	2
8								
		6	1		4	7		
								1
3	2				9		5	
4	6	9		1				
		8	4				2	

126

	8			3			7	
			2			3	8	
1			6	8		9		
						5	2	
3								7
	4	8						
		5		7	3			9
	7	2			9			
	3			1			5	

127

				9	8	7		
	6			3	5			
9		5						
5	3						4	
	1		4	6	3		7	
	7						3	2
						8		1
			3	7			6	
		1	8	5				

128

	8			5	3	6		
	5				7	2		
		9	4				8	
	4	1			8			
				1				
			2			8	4	
	3				5	1		
		5	6				2	
		7	3	8			6	

		1	8		6		2	3
2								5
	8		5					
	6			8				2
	9		1		3		5	
4				5			7	
					7		6	
5								4
1	4		9		5	2		

3				4		1	8	5
	5				6	4		3
5			2	7		3		
8	2						7	1
		3		8	1			9
1		7	3				5	
2	3	8		9				4

			5			1		
5			2			9		7
			3	4	9			
9					4	6		5
		8				4		
4		5	7					2
			9	3	2			
8		9			6			1
		3			5			

9					8			2
				6		1		
6					4	9	8	
	1				3			8
				5				
4			8				7	
	4	8	2					7
		9		4				
3			7					5

Puzzle 133

		5						
	9			5	1			4
4	6				2		8	
1				3				
	7						9	
				2				5
	4		3				1	9
6			9	1			7	
						6		

Puzzle 134

	6				2		4	
8		2	6					
				3	5			
		9	7			6		
7		4	8			3		1
	1		4			8		
		8	5					
				8	6			5
	9		4				8	

135

			7				6	
			3					9
1	8				2	5		
6						7	1	
9		7		3		8		2
	1	8						6
		2	4				9	8
4					1			
	9				7			

136

4						8	3	2
					2	4		
			6		3		5	
9					7	5		
		5		1		9		
		8	5					4
	6		8		4			
		1	2					
3	7	4						8

Puzzle 137

		4		9				3
	6	7			2	4		1
					4			
	7		6			8		4
		2				5		
4		5			8		2	
			2					
5		6	1			9	8	
1				8		3		

Puzzle 138

					6		2	
		4		5			8	1
			1		3			5
	2						4	
6		8		4		3		7
	4						5	
8			6		7			
1	6			9		8		
	5		3					

				3	9	2		
	8		6					7
		3	2					
1							5	4
2		7				9		8
9	5							2
					2	6		
8					6		7	
		4	3	5				

	6	5		1				
			9	5				2
		4					5	9
3			8					
1		7				9		4
					7			3
5	8					4		
7				4	9			
				7		2	9	

3	1	5			9			2
			5		3		4	
7				9			5	
8								9
	6			4				1
	7		2		6			
4			7			2	9	5

	4		1				8	5
				2		1		
		1			9	6		
4		8			2			
1	5						4	9
			8			3		1
		3	2			4		
		9		8				
7	8				6		1	

2			1					8
	1		7	4				
	6			8			7	1
9						7		
	7	1				3	8	
		3						6
7	5			9			6	
				5	8		9	
3					7			5

	1				5	8	2	
6				1				
5	4					1		
1			6					4
		9		5		6		
2					3			1
		1					6	9
				7				2
	2	7	3				1	

3	1						8	
				3	7			1
				9	7	6		
9		2			3			
1	3						7	2
			7			9		4
	6	9	4					
7			6	9				
	2						9	6

6			7					
				5		4		6
	1		6		2		9	
		4	1					
3			9	2	8			1
					5	3		
	8		5		9		7	
5		7		6				
					7			2

Puzzle 147

					1	4	3	
	3		7	8				
2			4					1
				1			9	
9	5						1	7
	7			5				
5					3			6
				4	9		7	
	1	8	5					

Puzzle 148

5							3	
			1	7				8
	1		2				6	
				5				7
	4	3				9	5	
6				4				
	9				7		1	
7				8	6			
	6							9

78

149

		8			5			2
			1		3	5	9	
9						8		
4	6	9						
		1				9		
						1	5	6
		4						8
	3	5	7		1			
6			9			3		

150

					3		8	9
5			9	1	6		7	
		3						
	1				7		4	
4								7
	5		2				6	
						8		
	4		1	7	8			6
3	9		5					

151

		7	1				8	
		3			6			
				3			4	6
2							9	7
			2	8	9			
9	5							1
3	9			7				
			8			9		
	4				2	3		

152

	4			3	8		9	5
2			9					
		3		5				4
	3	2						
			7	6	3			
						3	4	
3				8		7		
					1			6
6	8		4	7			5	

153

					5			9
					8	3		
4	1			3				6
		3			7			
5	6			4			1	7
			6			4		
6				7			8	2
		2	8					
9			1					

154

			6					1
				7	5			3
		8	1			6	7	
	5				2	1		
	4	2				8	6	
		1	9				2	
	2	4			1	9		
5			4	2				
1					9			

						4		9
	9		3	2			1	
			9			5		
		2	8			6		
8			6		7			4
		6			2	9		
		4			6			
	7			5	3		8	
3		1						

2						9	7	
6					2	4	3	
				8	7			
3				9			2	
7	2						9	4
	5			4				3
			8	5				
	6	7	4					1
	8	2						9

	4				3		7	
		1	6	7			8	2
				2		1		
6	5							
							1	8
		8		4				
4	9			6	1	5		
	1		2				3	

		4						
					6	1		5
			1	2		7		9
			7	5			3	2
	3			4			1	
1	6			3	2			
3		1		9	5			
8		9	2					
						4		

Puzzle 159

				1	9		2	
2	3		7	4				
			5			4		
	8	2						1
	4						6	
6						7	4	
		1			6			
				8	5		3	6
	2		3	7				

Puzzle 160

		6			3			
	3	7	5		9			
	1				7	4		
2	6				5			
	9						1	
			2				4	6
		1	3				7	
			9		1	6	8	
			7			9		

	1							8
	9				1	4	6	
		3	7				1	
				6	9			5
	2						4	
7			3	2				
	7				8	9		
	3	2	4				5	
4							8	

	9				2			6
		5				4		1
			9	8				
		4		2	3			
	7						2	
			7	4		3		
				7	8			
2		8				7		
5			4				6	

	7			4	6		9	
	9	3	7			6		
			3			4	8	
	1							
		8	9	1	3	7		
							6	
	8	9		6				
		7			5	8	2	
	2		3	7			1	

	1		4		7		5	
4		5			9		8	
			5					4
			3				7	6
3			6	4	5			1
1	8		9					
9			7					
	6		8			1		5
	5		9		1		3	

Puzzle 165:

		5		2		9		
6			5		1		3	
	4							
		6	3					4
	9	7				5	8	
3					7	2		
							7	
	1		7		5			2
		2		1		4		

Puzzle 166:

6				5	3			8
2							9	
	1				6			3
				2		3		
		4		9		5		
		6		8				
9			4				1	
	7							6
4			8	6				5

87

			4				6	8
	2			9		3		
3		5			1		9	
7		2			3			
			9			1		3
	3		5			9		6
		7		4			2	
5	1				2			

	3			2		4		
		4			8		6	5
					6		7	2
3				8				
8	1	2				5	3	7
				5				1
7	8		9					
1	2		8			7		
		3		7			2	

169

	3				8		4	
					4			
1	7		9	2			8	
		7	3			8	6	
6								4
	8	9				1	7	
	4			1	2		3	8
			6					
	1		8				7	

170

						7		8
2	6			8	9			
			3	6			2	
		4	5				7	
		7		9		2		
	1				7	4		
	3			4	5			
			8	7			4	6
8		1						

			3				2	4
	2			1		7		
	4	5	8					
5							6	9
				5				
1	3							8
					3	9	7	
		6		2			3	
4	9				1			

	3				4	7		1
5		2		8	7			
				2				8
3			5					
	6			3			4	
					1			7
4				9				
			8	1		4		3
6		8	4				5	

173

	3			8	9		6	
			7			4	1	
	5		2					7
	6		9		1			8
	7						5	
4			5		7		9	
1					3		2	
	4	7			2			
	2		6	9			7	

174

	1	8		7				9
						2		
	7		3		9		4	
5				3			7	
		9		6		5		
	3			4				8
	2		6		1		3	
		4						
8				5		7	9	

					3	9		1
	5						8	
8			4	1				
		1	9	6		3		
	7						6	
		9		7	4	5		
				4	6			5
	2						7	
7		6	3					

					2		1	6
2	8			6		3		
1		7			3		5	
		9						3
8				3				4
6						5		
	1		8			7		5
		6		1			9	8
9	5		6					

	1		2			4		
7					4			
		3		7		6		1
8							1	
	5			8			2	
	7							3
6		5		3		2		
			4					8
		9			2		3	

	1	8	6	5			4	
6								7
4							8	
9	4			3	6			
			7		2			
			1	8			9	3
	6							5
8								1
	2			1	3	9	7	

		4						
3		5		1	9	6		
	9			5			7	3
	2	3		6	7		8	
	5		2	8		3	6	
6	1			7			9	
		8	6	9		2		4
						7		

4			6		8	2		
6		2						4
	5						9	
			4	3		5		1
			1		2			
1		8		5	6			
	2						1	
5						7		9
		6	9		4			2

181

7		9				5	1	
2			7					
3		8	6			7		
		7			4			
			3		1			
			8			3		
		5			9	6		3
					6			4
	9	4				2		5

182

7					8			
						9	6	
		1	5	3		8	4	
6					9		5	
				5				
	5		1					3
	4	6		2	7	3		
	8	3						
			4					9

			1		4			
		7		3		9		6
	3			9	5	2		
					2			4
9	1	3				8	2	7
2			3					
		6	5	4			8	
4		2		1		5		
			8		9			

				2			1	
8	3	2						4
			6		9			7
		8	5	7		9		2
7		9		8	2	4		
4			2		3			
6						1	2	8
	9			5				

	2					8		7
7			6					
9					2	1		
1	8		4		9			
				6				
			7		5		4	1
		7	5					8
					3			9
2		1					6	

	8	3		5				
						2	4	
		9	7	2	3			6
			1			9		2
				4				
8		7			5			
9			5	7	8	3		
	7	6						
				3		7	2	

			2	9		3	7	
			1				6	
				7		2	9	1
	6	1			4		3	
	8						1	
	3		6			7	5	
7	9	6		4				
	4				2			
	2	3		6	7			

1	6		7					3
7		5		8		2		
			9				6	
						1		5
	3			2			7	
5		1						
	4				8			
		7		9		4		2
6					5		3	9

6						5	9	
	4							
2			9	7				1
4		2			9	6		
				1				
		1	7			4		3
1				8	2			4
							6	
	9	3						5

		3	7					4
4	9					5		
7	1				2			
2			3		7			
		9				8		
			4		1			2
			1				3	8
		6					7	9
3					9	4		

			1				5	8
		8	5	9	3			2
		1		6				
2		4	7					9
				3				
5					1	2		7
				1		9		
1			9	5	8	3		
9	4				6			

	2	1						
		8				9	1	
	7		8		9	4		
				4	8			3
	1						5	
6			7	5				
		2	5		1		6	
	3	9				1		
						2	8	

193

	2	5						
	8				1	5	3	2
1	6					7		
				6	2		4	
			8		5			
	3		7	9				
		9					7	5
6	5	2	1				8	
						4	2	

194

2			8	9				
4		7			3			
	8							
		5	1			4		2
9		4	7		5	8		3
3		6			8	9		
							8	
			3			1		6
				7	2			9

5		6						
	9	7						5
			6	3				2
	3				1			
2			7		9			8
			4				6	
7				8	6			
8						9	4	
						8		1

		2						
		6			9			8
	1		6	2		5		
2		1			5		7	
	5		2		6		9	
	4		7			8		5
		7		6	4		1	
1			9			7		
						9		

		9	8		3	1		
5								
				7	6		8	
9		8	6					3
1								5
2					4	8		6
	6		7	4				
								2
		2	3		5	6		

	4				9	2		
3					6			7
		7		5	1			
	8				7	9		
		3				4		
		4	6				3	
			5	8		7		
8			7					1
		2	1				4	

1				3			6	
5					9	7		
					7	4	2	
		5				1		
			8	7	4			
		6				8		
	8	9	7					
		1	2					4
	2			5				1

5					3	9	6	
6			5					
		1			2			5
	8		3				7	1
		5				3		
3	1				7		5	
4			7			2		
					8			4
	9	7	2					3

	5		6			4	8	
4						2		
7			1					
			6			1		2
9			5					6
2		4	7					
				8				4
		3						9
	7	9			4		6	

2	6			1		9		
			2		4		3	
					7			8
	4	1						6
		5	4		3	1		
6						4	5	
8			7					
	5		3		8			
		6		5			4	2

	2			9	7			6
9						2		
		5	8				9	
		7						
		9	2	8	5	3		
						4		
	6				4	9		
		3						2
2			6	1			3	

		6	1	3				
	7			8				2
	9			7	4			
		2			3	6		
9		4				1		7
		8	7			2		
			3	2			1	
6				1			9	
				6	7	8		

				6	8			
1		5						
2	3	8			4			6
9				8		3		
	1						8	
		7		3				4
6			4			1	9	7
						6		3
			9	2				

4					7		3	
6		2					8	
	3				8			
	1	4	5					
3				8				9
					1	2	4	
			1				5	
	2					3		7
	5		3					8

207

					5	6		
4		1	7			2		
8				6			7	
			9	6				
5	1	2				4	9	6
			2	5				
	7			4				2
		5			3	1		7
		6	9					

208

9	2	7		6			1	
					7			
		8	3	4				2
	4			7				8
		9	1		4	7		
7				2			4	
4				8	2	5		
			6					
	8			5		2	6	7

209

		8	1				2	
		6		2			5	7
2	9			4		3		
	8							
	7		3	6	5		4	
							9	
		4		5			8	9
7	6			8		4		
	2				4	7		

210

6	1	5		7				
			6	5	2			
	3							
9			1			3	4	
5								7
	4	2			7			1
							7	
			4	1	9			
				2		1	5	8

5								
				1		6	3	
2	6		7					8
		9	8					7
1			9		6			2
4					1	3		
8					5		7	1
	9	2		4				
								6

5						6		
6	4	9	5					8
					1		5	
	8	7	2	4				
				1	7	9	2	
	9		1					
4					2	8	3	5
		3						9

213

	8				1			7
		5			3			
2		3					9	
	4		1	8		2		6
6		1		4	9		8	
	5					8		9
			3			4		
8			6				1	

214

			5					6
		4		1				9
		6	8	9		7		
	9	3				2	7	
			6		7			
	5	7				6	4	
		9		6	8	3		
7				3		4		
2					1			

215

			2			5	3	
				8			6	
			7	9		4		2
	6	5						1
		2				6		
1						8	4	
5		8		7	9			
	7			3				
	4	1			8			

216

6	3	1	7				8	
			6		1			
				5		3		
	8				6			9
	1			9			7	
5			1				4	
		5		1				
			8		4			
	9				5	8	2	1

Puzzle 217

9		7	1			4		8
		5		3	7			
	3							
	9							4
			9	6	3			
2							5	
							8	
			4	7		1		
1		6			2	9		3

Puzzle 218

3					4	7		1
4			6				9	
6				7				
							3	4
	6		1		9		5	
5	1							
				8				3
	8				2			5
7		2	9					6

219

1			7					6
	4	3	1		6			2
	6			9				
								1
		9	8	6	7	3		
4								
				7			5	
9			4		8	1	6	
7					9			3

220

					7	9		6
		6	2			3		
			4					7
	3			7				8
1	6			9			7	4
9				2		3		
2					1			
		5			3	1		
6			1	9				

		4			1	9		
	9			3		1	6	
		6	9	7			8	
				1			9	
			7		6			
	7			4				
	4			9	5	3		
	2	5		8			4	
		9	1			5		

	9			8		1		
8	5				4			
		1	6					2
								8
3			4		6			7
9								
2					1	8		
			7				2	3
		7		5			4	

Puzzle 223 and 224

2 2 3

	6				1		7	9
		2	6			4		
		9		4				
	8							3
			2	1	3			
7							6	
				6		9		
		7			2	3		
2	3		8				5	

2 2 4

3	6							2
		9	1					7
						4	9	
9			2		4	7		
2			5	6	7			8
		6	3		9			1
	9	8						
7					1	6		
1							3	9

		7	4			2	9	
	5		6			4		1
		2					8	
		3		5	2		1	
				1				
	2		8	6		7		
	3					9		
9		5			6		3	
	7	6			8	1		

		9			5	6		3
			9	6				7
			1			5		
7	2	5	6					
	8						4	
					3	5	2	8
	6			3				
4				5	7			
1		7	8			2		

		7	1			8		
					3	7	1	
8								6
7	2		9					
	5	3	4		7	6	9	
					5		7	3
4								9
	1	6	2					
		5			1	4		

			7					
		9			3	5		
2	4			9				
	9				2	6		8
		6		5		1		
1		3	6				2	
				8			5	3
		5	3			9		
					1			

229

			3			5		
5				2	9	4		1
		9				8		
2	7			4				
				1				
				9			2	7
		3				7		
6		7	5	3				8
		5			1			

230

9			1			7		
		7			9		2	8
	2			6				
				3				5
			5		8			
7				4				
				2			5	
6	4		9			1		
		3			4			6

			3		8		4	1
			6	7		3		8
						9		
2							8	7
		1		8		6		
6	3							4
		6						
4		9		3	2			
1	7		4		6			

				8			6	
			7			3	1	
1	5	4						7
4	7			3				2
3				5			9	6
7						2	4	3
	4	6			3			
	8			1				

233

8		2		5				
	5				9		6	
		4	2				3	
		7	6					8
2								9
4					8	6		
	4				2	1		
	3		9				7	
				3		4		6

234

	5	9			1		4	
				2		6		
			4	3		2	1	
						9	3	8
7	3	4						
	1	7		9	6			
		5		4				
	6		8			4	5	

				8				
1		9					6	
	8				6		1	9
3					4	5		
			7	3	9			
		4	5					1
9	7		4				5	
	4					2		7
				5				

	7			8	4		1	
				2				7
			3			2	4	
		6			5	7		
3		2		7		6		1
		7	1			9		
	6	5			3			
9				6				
	3		9	5			6	

7	5	1						
	6							
3				7	6			
6				4		2		7
		7	3		2	9		
1		2		8				5
			1	9				8
							5	
						4	1	2

	3				8			
			9			1	7	3
		5		7				
8	5					7		
			8	4	3			
		1					4	2
				8		4		
7	1	2			9			
			1				5	

239

		2		5		3	8	
4				3		2		
8			4					
	7	3						
			9	8	4			
						9	6	
					6			8
		5		2				6
	6	9		4		7		

240

1			9				6	5
	7					9		
				8		2	1	
		5			2		8	4
				4				
3	1		7			5		
	4	7		2				
		1					5	
5	8				7			6

241

			7	3				
	5		9					
3	2	8				7		
		3						2
7	8						3	6
6						1		
		9				4	7	1
					4		6	
				7	5			

242

6		2					7	
	9			7	4			
7			8		6			
					8	4	3	
5								9
	4	7	6					
			2		1			8
			3	8			5	
	1					6		3

Puzzle 243

	7			6			8	5
4		8	2		7			
2								7
				8	4		7	
	9						1	
	4		6	2				
7								1
			8		2	7		3
5	2			3			4	

Puzzle 244

		8		2	4			1
	3		9				2	
								7
6					3		7	5
			5		1			
5	2		8					9
8								
	5				8		4	
3			7	1		6		

126

3	9		6			8		
			8		2		1	
	1			3			6	7
				9	7			8
		8				1		
5			1	2				
7	2			4			8	
	3		7		9			
		5			3		7	9

				5		7		
4			9	3			5	1
1	2							3
6	1		2					
8								4
					6		1	8
9							4	6
2	4			6	9			5
		8		2				

						3		
3					5	8		2
		9		2	8		4	
5							8	
			4		6			
	6							1
	8		9	1		7		
6		4	5					9
		5						

9	8		1			4		3
			9				8	
					4			7
2				9		1		8
	5						2	
1		8		6				4
7			5					
	3				2			
8		4			9		5	2

Puzzle 249:

2			6	7		9	8	
		9						6
		1					2	4
					5		9	
			1		6			
	1		7					
6	7					3		
3						2		
	9	5		4	2			7

Puzzle 250:

				2			1	
			4			3		
	7		8		1	2		4
		5	9				3	
6		2				5		7
	3				2	1		
2		1	7		9		4	
		4			5			
	5			8				

1				4				
	4	2	1			7	5	3
	5	8						
4			9		6	1		
7								9
		1	3		5			4
						2	4	
8	2	6				1	9	7
				9				6

						4		
6	8				1		2	
1		7		6			9	
			5				8	4
		8				1		
3	2				7			
	7			4		2		5
	5		2				1	7
		2						

253

				5	1	3		
			6					8
	7	2	4					9
							7	
6		8				4		1
	3							
2					9	6	5	
8					6			
		7	5	2				

254

				7			9	
4							3	5
7		5						
					5	2	4	
			2		8			
	8	3	6					
						9		7
3	9							2
	7			4				

	4			2		3		
8			3			9		
3	6		4					
9			2			7		8
6		4			5			2
					9		3	5
		7			2			9
		3		1			6	

	1		2					3
		3				4	7	
			5			2		
6		9	1	5	2		4	
	4		3	6	8	9		2
		6			1			
	3	4				7		
5					9		1	

	9		5		3			8
2		7				5		
		1	6					
3				6	9	4		
			7		2			
		6	3	8				7
					4	8		
		3				2		4
7			2		6		3	

		2	6					
						7		
5	9	8		2			6	
				9	5		8	
		3	4		2	5		
	2		3	7				
	6			4		1	9	2
		4						
					7	8		

259

	4		6					
		5	8	7				
6	2						8	
7						2	6	
1		2				7		5
	3	9						8
	5						9	3
				2	1	5		
					5		2	

260

			5					
	9		1			6		
				3	2		8	9
	5	8			1		7	
4			3		6			2
	6		7			9	5	
6	1		4	2				
		4			7		2	
					5			

261

				3	6	9	8	5
			1			2		7
		3						4
2					5			
		9				6		
			7					2
9						3		
8		7			1			
6	5	4	3	2				

262

		6	1					4
							8	2
	2			9	4	1		
9			5			7		
	8			4			3	
		1			9			6
		8	9	3			5	
1	9							
7					2	6		

6							4	
		7	6			3		8
			7		5		1	
			8				9	2
		1				4		
9	7				3			
	6		2		7			
3		4			6	1		
	9							4

					7	5	9	
		6		1				4
		4	8				2	
8	7							
				5				
							3	1
	5				9	8		
1				3		9		
	2	3	6					

265

								5
	8		6	5			7	2
5	9							
	3		8		4			
7		2				8		1
			2		3		6	
							1	7
3	7			2	5		8	
9								

266

		4			9		1	
				2	6	5		
6	1						3	
			2		8	1		6
				4				
9		8	6		7			
	4						5	1
		5	4	8				
	3		9			4		

		7	6				3	
3						9		4
	2	4		1		7		
8		1	7				5	
	9				8	3		7
		2		4		8	7	
6		9						3
	8				7	5		

5		4		3		2		1
	8						4	
					1			6
3			6				2	
1								9
	4				7			3
9			1					
	3						1	
7		2		9		5		4

269

5		1				8	4	
7	4			5				
	3				4			
		9	2				1	
		4	8		9	3		
	8				1	9		
			7				8	
				2			7	3
	7	3				6		9

270

			4		3			
	4	2	1					
	1	6		8				3
9		5				7	1	
6								2
	7	1				3		5
1				5		2	7	
					9	8	3	
			7		4			

Puzzle 271

5	2				1			3
			2	9				
	4						8	
4					3	7	6	
		7				3		
	9	2	5					1
	6						3	
				1	9			
2			8				5	4

Puzzle 272

					3	8		
6			4			7	5	3
				9				1
		8			5			
	7	2				5	8	
			9			2		
1				7				
2	4	5			9			6
		6	2					

6		2	3			5		
			6	1	4			
	1					3		6
5		8	2					
	2			3			9	
					8	4		5
2		7					5	
			7	9	6			
		9			2	7		4

					2			
7		8			5			
9	2					4	3	
		4		6			8	3
	3						1	
2	8			3		9		
	1	3					4	7
			5			1		9
			4					

						3	1	
7	5			4				8
		1	7					2
					8	4		3
				6				
2		5	1					
5					7	1		
1				8			6	5
	3	6						

5				1	9			2
4	8	9			3		1	6
3	2					6		
			5		2			
		7					9	3
7	3		8			9	2	4
8			3	2				1

					3	4		
					1		9	6
1	6			2			8	
5		2	8					
	9						6	
					2	3		7
	4			7			1	2
6	2		1					
		9	2					

					9	2		6
9	3			1		6		
		7	5				9	
4	8					3		
		3				9		
		9					7	8
	7				1	5		
			3		2		6	1
2		4	6					

279

						6		
	4	7		5		8		
		8			3		5	
		6		7			1	
	3		1		9		6	
	9			8		2		
	5		4			1		
		1		6		9	3	
		4						

280

			8					
8		1		9				
	5		2		3			9
7	2						3	
		5	7		6	1		
	3						7	8
3			9		2		4	
				5		2		6
					4			

281

			9			3		7
4	7				2		5	
	9	1				8		
6		4	2				3	
				9				
	8				3	2		4
		7				6	1	
	4		5				9	2
2		9			1			

282

	2				4			7
						1	6	
6		4		1		5		
	9			6	2			
1				4				2
			9	8			5	
		8		7		4		5
	6	7						
2			5				7	

283

		4	5			8		
			6		2	3	9	
		7					5	
			3			1		
				5				
		8			9			
	8					7		
	3	5	2		8			
		2			1	9		

284

					8		6	4
	3		2					
		9			1	8		
				7		4		
8	9						7	3
		2		1				
		1	4			5		
					3		8	
5	6		1					

		9			3	7		
5					6		2	
			2	5				1
		4					8	
			3	9	4			
	3					9		
1				3	9			
	7		8					5
		5	6			1		

			4	5				
		5	9		7			8
							9	1
	4		7			1	2	
5								7
	3	7			9		4	
4	1							
9			5		3	2		
				2	4			

287

4	9						6	7
	8				1			
		1		5				
						6	4	1
				3				
9	2	8						
				4		3		
			9				5	
2	3						9	4

288

		8		4		7		
		3		8	2			
	1		9					4
4		9	1					
3								7
					7	6		3
9					4		2	
			6	2		1		
		7		1		3		

289

2				5		6		
			2		8			1
3		5					2	
		9			5		7	2
				4				
4	8		3			9		
	2					5		7
1			5		9			
		7		2				4

290

		5	3				6	2
				4	2			
1		9					4	
5						2	7	
				6				
	3	7						9
	9					4		1
			8	3				
3	5				1	6		

291

			3		4			6
4				1				
7	2				9	1		
	7				2		9	3
		2				7		
9	1		6				5	
		5	7				1	2
				3				9
2			4		5			

292

		7	3	9		1		
								6
	6					8	7	
4	7		5	3			1	
	1			4			3	
	3			6	2		8	7
	9	3					2	
7								
		1		2	3	5		

293

7		6				2		1
2	4					6		
				6	2	3		
4				1	6			
	3		9		8		1	
			3	4				2
		7	8	3				
		4					9	8
8		9				1		6

294

2							9	8
		5	1	9				
	4		8	3				7
		8			5			
3				8				6
			4			7		
5				4	8		6	
				1	9	2		
4	3							9

Puzzle 295

			3		5		4	7
2					4			8
			9			6		
					9		5	
8				6				1
	4		7					
		8			3			
9			4					5
5	2		1		6			

Puzzle 296

		1	9		6			5
		6	1			3	4	
				7				
	7						9	3
9			2		3			6
6	5						1	
				3				
	9	5			4	6		
4			6		9	2		

			1		4		9	5
	1			2	5			7
		4	7			1		
7				9			1	
	6			1				3
		3			2	5		
2			4	5			8	
5	4		3		8			

	4		1		7			
			6		5		9	
5						4	2	1
2						5		
7	1		5		2		8	3
		8						2
3	9	1						8
	2		9		8			
			3		4		5	

								6
9		6	5					
	5			4	1		7	
5			9		4		6	
	7			1			3	
	9		3		5			7
	3		1	5			4	
					9	3		2
1								

2				9				
	5				2	7		
9	6		7			1		
6			1	4				
			9		3			
			5	7				8
		3			6		4	2
		6	4				3	
			2					5

1

7	1	8	3	9	4	5	6	2
5	2	4	1	8	6	9	7	3
3	9	6	5	7	2	1	4	8
8	5	1	6	4	7	2	3	9
9	3	7	8	2	5	4	1	6
6	4	2	9	3	1	8	5	7
1	8	3	7	5	9	6	2	4
4	7	5	2	6	8	3	9	1
2	6	9	4	1	3	7	8	5

2

2	3	7	1	6	9	5	8	4
9	8	1	2	5	4	7	6	3
5	6	4	8	3	7	1	2	9
6	5	8	4	1	2	9	3	7
3	1	2	9	7	5	8	4	6
7	4	9	3	8	6	2	1	5
1	7	5	6	2	3	4	9	8
8	9	6	7	4	1	3	5	2
4	2	3	5	9	8	6	7	1

3

1	2	3	5	6	7	8	4	9
8	6	4	2	3	9	5	7	1
7	5	9	1	4	8	6	2	3
9	4	5	3	7	6	1	8	2
3	1	6	9	8	2	4	5	7
2	7	8	4	5	1	9	3	6
6	8	1	7	2	4	3	9	5
5	9	7	8	1	3	2	6	4
4	3	2	6	9	5	7	1	8

4

9	8	2	3	1	5	6	7	4
5	6	4	8	7	2	9	3	1
1	3	7	9	6	4	5	2	8
6	4	3	7	5	9	8	1	2
7	1	5	6	2	8	3	4	9
8	2	9	4	3	1	7	6	5
2	9	6	5	4	7	1	8	3
3	5	1	2	8	6	4	9	7
4	7	8	1	9	3	2	5	6

5

3	8	9	4	5	1	6	2	7
6	2	7	8	3	9	5	1	4
5	1	4	6	7	2	3	9	8
4	3	8	1	6	7	2	5	9
1	6	5	2	9	8	4	7	3
7	9	2	5	4	3	1	8	6
8	5	6	7	1	4	9	3	2
9	7	1	3	2	6	8	4	5
2	4	3	9	8	5	7	6	1

6

8	2	1	7	5	6	4	9	3
6	4	3	8	1	9	2	7	5
7	9	5	3	2	4	1	6	8
3	8	2	9	7	1	5	4	6
1	7	9	4	6	5	8	3	2
5	6	4	2	3	8	9	1	7
4	3	7	1	8	2	6	5	9
2	1	6	5	9	7	3	8	4
9	5	8	6	4	3	7	2	1

7

7	8	4	3	1	2	9	6	5
5	3	1	7	6	9	4	8	2
6	2	9	5	8	4	3	7	1
1	5	7	8	2	3	6	9	4
9	4	2	6	5	7	8	1	3
3	6	8	4	9	1	2	5	7
2	7	5	9	3	6	1	4	8
4	1	6	2	7	8	5	3	9
8	9	3	1	4	5	7	2	6

8

3	8	2	7	6	5	1	4	9
7	9	5	4	3	1	6	2	8
1	6	4	9	8	2	5	7	3
4	5	3	8	2	7	9	1	6
2	7	9	3	1	6	4	8	5
6	1	8	5	4	9	2	3	7
9	4	7	2	5	3	8	6	1
5	2	6	1	7	8	3	9	4
8	3	1	6	9	4	7	5	2

9

2	3	7	4	8	6	9	1	5
9	4	5	3	1	2	8	7	6
6	8	1	9	7	5	4	3	2
5	9	8	1	2	4	3	6	7
4	6	2	5	3	7	1	8	9
1	7	3	6	9	8	5	2	4
7	2	9	8	5	3	6	4	1
3	1	6	2	4	9	7	5	8
8	5	4	7	6	1	2	9	3

10

7	1	4	2	8	5	9	6	3
8	6	9	7	4	3	2	5	1
3	2	5	6	1	9	7	4	8
1	4	3	8	2	6	5	7	9
6	5	2	1	9	7	3	8	4
9	8	7	3	5	4	6	1	2
5	9	6	4	3	8	1	2	7
4	3	1	5	7	2	8	9	6
2	7	8	9	6	1	4	3	5

11

8	9	1	5	4	2	3	6	7
4	7	6	3	8	9	2	1	5
3	5	2	7	6	1	4	9	8
6	8	4	9	1	3	7	5	2
9	2	3	4	5	7	1	8	6
7	1	5	8	2	6	9	3	4
2	6	7	1	9	8	5	4	3
5	3	9	6	7	4	8	2	1
1	4	8	2	3	5	6	7	9

12

3	4	7	1	5	2	6	9	8
1	9	8	7	3	6	2	5	4
2	5	6	8	9	4	7	1	3
6	7	3	4	1	8	9	2	5
5	2	1	3	6	9	4	8	7
9	8	4	2	7	5	1	3	6
8	3	9	6	2	7	5	4	1
4	6	2	5	8	1	3	7	9
7	1	5	9	4	3	8	6	2

13

8	1	2	9	4	3	7	5	6
7	6	4	2	8	5	1	9	3
3	5	9	6	1	7	2	4	8
4	8	1	5	7	6	3	2	9
6	3	5	8	9	2	4	1	7
9	2	7	4	3	1	6	8	5
5	4	3	7	2	9	8	6	1
2	7	6	1	5	8	9	3	4
1	9	8	3	6	4	5	7	2

14

8	9	1	2	4	5	6	3	7
5	6	7	8	9	3	4	1	2
3	2	4	1	7	6	5	8	9
6	1	8	5	3	2	7	9	4
7	5	2	9	8	4	3	6	1
4	3	9	6	1	7	8	2	5
9	8	5	4	6	1	2	7	3
2	7	6	3	5	9	1	4	8
1	4	3	7	2	8	9	5	6

15

7	5	4	9	3	8	2	6	1
6	3	9	2	7	1	4	8	5
8	1	2	5	4	6	3	7	9
9	8	7	4	6	5	1	3	2
1	4	3	8	2	9	6	5	7
2	6	5	7	1	3	8	9	4
3	7	6	1	9	2	5	4	8
4	2	8	3	5	7	9	1	6
5	9	1	6	8	4	7	2	3

16

4	2	6	9	5	7	3	1	8
1	5	3	2	8	6	7	9	4
9	8	7	4	3	1	5	6	2
3	1	5	7	2	8	9	4	6
2	6	4	3	1	9	8	5	7
7	9	8	5	6	4	1	2	3
8	3	1	6	4	5	2	7	9
6	7	2	1	9	3	4	8	5
5	4	9	8	7	2	6	3	1

17

3	8	4	5	9	6	7	1	2
5	2	7	1	8	4	9	6	3
9	6	1	2	7	3	4	8	5
1	9	8	7	4	5	2	3	6
2	7	6	9	3	8	5	4	1
4	5	3	6	2	1	8	9	7
6	4	9	3	5	2	1	7	8
7	3	2	8	1	9	6	5	4
8	1	5	4	6	7	3	2	9

18

5	2	6	1	3	8	4	9	7
4	1	9	5	6	7	2	3	8
3	7	8	9	4	2	6	1	5
1	5	7	3	2	6	8	4	9
6	3	2	4	8	9	5	7	1
8	9	4	7	5	1	3	2	6
9	6	3	2	7	5	1	8	4
2	8	1	6	9	4	7	5	3
7	4	5	8	1	3	9	6	2

19

3	2	6	5	4	9	8	1	7
7	9	1	3	8	2	6	4	5
5	4	8	1	7	6	2	9	3
4	1	3	7	5	8	9	6	2
2	8	7	6	9	3	4	5	1
9	6	5	4	2	1	3	7	8
8	7	9	2	1	4	5	3	6
6	5	4	8	3	7	1	2	9
1	3	2	9	6	5	7	8	4

20

2	1	9	6	8	4	3	7	5
4	8	6	3	5	7	1	2	9
3	5	7	9	1	2	4	6	8
7	6	2	4	3	8	9	5	1
9	3	1	2	7	5	6	8	4
8	4	5	1	6	9	7	3	2
1	9	3	5	2	6	8	4	7
5	7	4	8	9	3	2	1	6
6	2	8	7	4	1	5	9	3

21

1	6	4	9	7	5	3	2	8
7	3	8	2	6	1	9	4	5
9	2	5	3	4	8	7	6	1
2	4	6	5	3	9	8	1	7
5	1	3	7	8	4	6	9	2
8	7	9	6	1	2	5	3	4
3	5	2	4	9	7	1	8	6
6	8	7	1	2	3	4	5	9
4	9	1	8	5	6	2	7	3

22

4	1	8	3	9	7	6	2	5
2	7	5	8	6	1	4	9	3
9	3	6	4	5	2	8	7	1
5	9	1	2	8	3	7	4	6
3	6	7	9	4	5	2	1	8
8	2	4	7	1	6	5	3	9
1	4	9	5	2	8	3	6	7
6	5	3	1	7	4	9	8	2
7	8	2	6	3	9	1	5	4

23

6	9	5	3	7	2	4	8	1
1	7	3	8	5	4	6	9	2
4	8	2	1	9	6	5	7	3
5	6	8	9	1	3	7	2	4
3	4	7	2	6	8	1	5	9
9	2	1	7	4	5	8	3	6
8	1	9	4	3	7	2	6	5
7	5	4	6	2	9	3	1	8
2	3	6	5	8	1	9	4	7

24

5	6	1	7	4	9	3	8	2
2	3	8	6	1	5	4	9	7
4	7	9	8	2	3	5	1	6
1	8	2	4	6	7	9	5	3
7	9	4	3	5	2	1	6	8
6	5	3	9	8	1	7	2	4
9	2	6	5	3	4	8	7	1
8	4	7	1	9	6	2	3	5
3	1	5	2	7	8	6	4	9

25

2	3	6	8	7	4	9	5	1
9	7	8	1	3	5	2	6	4
4	5	1	9	6	2	8	7	3
5	8	7	4	9	3	1	2	6
3	9	4	6	2	1	7	8	5
6	1	2	7	5	8	4	3	9
7	6	3	2	4	9	5	1	8
8	2	9	5	1	6	3	4	7
1	4	5	3	8	7	6	9	2

26

4	1	6	2	7	5	8	9	3
8	9	3	4	6	1	7	2	5
7	5	2	3	9	8	6	4	1
9	2	7	1	4	3	5	6	8
3	8	4	5	2	6	9	1	7
1	6	5	9	8	7	2	3	4
2	7	9	8	3	4	1	5	6
6	3	1	7	5	2	4	8	9
5	4	8	6	1	9	3	7	2

27

3	2	5	8	7	9	6	4	1
7	9	4	2	6	1	8	3	5
6	8	1	4	3	5	2	9	7
1	5	6	9	2	3	7	8	4
9	4	8	7	1	6	5	2	3
2	3	7	5	8	4	9	1	6
5	7	9	1	4	8	3	6	2
8	1	3	6	5	2	4	7	9
4	6	2	3	9	7	1	5	8

28

7	3	2	9	8	4	1	6	5
4	9	5	6	1	2	7	8	3
1	8	6	3	7	5	4	2	9
2	1	8	7	3	6	5	9	4
6	4	7	5	9	1	8	3	2
3	5	9	4	2	8	6	1	7
9	6	3	8	4	7	2	5	1
8	2	4	1	5	3	9	7	6
5	7	1	2	6	9	3	4	8

29

7	4	2	9	6	3	8	5	1
9	8	6	4	5	1	2	3	7
3	5	1	8	2	7	6	4	9
4	1	5	7	8	2	3	9	6
6	2	7	3	4	9	5	1	8
8	9	3	6	1	5	7	2	4
1	3	9	2	7	8	4	6	5
5	7	4	1	3	6	9	8	2
2	6	8	5	9	4	1	7	3

30

5	3	4	9	1	7	2	8	6
1	2	7	5	6	8	9	3	4
8	9	6	3	4	2	7	1	5
6	7	9	8	2	1	4	5	3
4	5	2	6	9	3	1	7	8
3	1	8	7	5	4	6	2	9
7	8	1	4	3	6	5	9	2
2	6	5	1	8	9	3	4	7
9	4	3	2	7	5	8	6	1

31

4	1	7	5	9	8	2	3	6
5	2	8	3	6	1	7	4	9
3	6	9	4	2	7	5	1	8
7	9	4	8	1	5	3	6	2
6	8	2	7	3	9	4	5	1
1	5	3	2	4	6	8	9	7
8	4	1	9	7	3	6	2	5
9	3	5	6	8	2	1	7	4
2	7	6	1	5	4	9	8	3

32

2	9	1	7	8	5	4	6	3
8	7	3	9	6	4	2	1	5
4	6	5	3	2	1	7	9	8
7	3	8	5	4	9	6	2	1
5	1	2	6	7	3	9	8	4
6	4	9	8	1	2	5	3	7
1	2	6	4	5	8	3	7	9
9	8	4	2	3	7	1	5	6
3	5	7	1	9	6	8	4	2

33

5	4	8	1	6	7	2	3	9
6	1	7	9	2	3	8	5	4
9	3	2	5	4	8	1	6	7
1	8	9	2	3	5	7	4	6
4	2	3	8	7	6	5	9	1
7	5	6	4	9	1	3	2	8
2	9	1	7	5	4	6	8	3
3	7	5	6	8	9	4	1	2
8	6	4	3	1	2	9	7	5

34

7	9	5	6	2	3	8	4	1
8	6	1	4	7	5	2	3	9
4	2	3	1	8	9	5	6	7
9	5	6	2	1	7	4	8	3
1	7	8	5	3	4	9	2	6
2	3	4	9	6	8	1	7	5
5	1	7	8	4	6	3	9	2
3	8	9	7	5	2	6	1	4
6	4	2	3	9	1	7	5	8

35

5	4	2	6	8	7	9	3	1
6	9	1	4	5	3	2	8	7
8	7	3	9	1	2	6	4	5
7	6	4	8	9	1	5	2	3
1	5	8	2	3	4	7	9	6
3	2	9	7	6	5	4	1	8
9	3	5	1	4	6	8	7	2
2	8	6	3	7	9	1	5	4
4	1	7	5	2	8	3	6	9

36

6	5	8	1	2	9	7	3	4
9	2	3	4	8	7	6	5	1
1	7	4	6	5	3	8	2	9
7	9	6	3	4	8	5	1	2
8	4	5	7	1	2	9	6	3
2	3	1	9	6	5	4	8	7
3	8	7	5	9	1	2	4	6
5	6	9	2	3	4	1	7	8
4	1	2	8	7	6	3	9	5

37

5	3	2	9	8	1	4	7	6
7	8	1	3	6	4	5	2	9
4	6	9	7	5	2	3	8	1
2	5	4	6	7	8	1	9	3
6	7	8	1	9	3	2	5	4
9	1	3	4	2	5	7	6	8
3	9	7	5	4	6	8	1	2
1	2	6	8	3	7	9	4	5
8	4	5	2	1	9	6	3	7

38

8	3	2	6	9	4	1	5	7
7	4	5	3	1	8	2	6	9
1	9	6	2	5	7	3	4	8
4	6	9	1	3	2	8	7	5
5	2	8	7	6	9	4	3	1
3	7	1	4	8	5	9	2	6
6	8	3	5	4	1	7	9	2
9	5	7	8	2	3	6	1	4
2	1	4	9	7	6	5	8	3

39

5	1	4	8	7	6	3	9	2
8	7	9	2	1	3	4	6	5
3	2	6	9	4	5	7	8	1
7	4	3	6	5	1	9	2	8
9	6	1	4	2	8	5	3	7
2	8	5	7	3	9	6	1	4
4	9	7	3	8	2	1	5	6
1	3	8	5	6	7	2	4	9
6	5	2	1	9	4	8	7	3

40

7	9	1	3	2	5	8	6	4
6	8	2	4	1	9	5	7	3
4	3	5	8	6	7	2	9	1
8	5	7	9	3	6	4	1	2
3	1	4	2	7	8	9	5	6
9	2	6	1	5	4	3	8	7
2	6	8	5	4	1	7	3	9
1	4	9	7	8	3	6	2	5
5	7	3	6	9	2	1	4	8

4-1

6	5	2	1	9	7	4	8	3
4	9	1	3	2	8	7	5	6
8	7	3	6	5	4	1	2	9
3	8	6	4	7	2	5	9	1
9	1	5	8	6	3	2	4	7
7	2	4	5	1	9	6	3	8
5	3	7	2	8	1	9	6	4
2	4	9	7	3	6	8	1	5
1	6	8	9	4	5	3	7	2

4-2

1	9	4	8	3	7	5	6	2
8	7	5	9	6	2	3	1	4
3	2	6	1	5	4	8	9	7
2	1	7	5	8	9	4	3	6
4	8	9	6	7	3	2	5	1
6	5	3	4	2	1	9	7	8
7	4	2	3	9	6	1	8	5
5	3	1	7	4	8	6	2	9
9	6	8	2	1	5	7	4	3

4-3

5	6	1	3	2	8	9	4	7
7	2	8	1	9	4	6	5	3
4	9	3	7	5	6	1	8	2
6	7	4	9	8	1	3	2	5
1	3	9	2	4	5	8	7	6
2	8	5	6	7	3	4	1	9
3	5	6	8	1	2	7	9	4
8	4	7	5	6	9	2	3	1
9	1	2	4	3	7	5	6	8

4-4

2	9	4	8	5	3	7	6	1
5	7	1	4	9	6	2	8	3
6	8	3	1	2	7	4	9	5
1	5	6	7	8	9	3	2	4
8	3	2	5	4	1	6	7	9
7	4	9	6	3	2	5	1	8
4	6	8	2	1	5	9	3	7
9	2	5	3	7	8	1	4	6
3	1	7	9	6	4	8	5	2

4-5

2	5	4	3	8	1	9	6	7
7	8	9	2	4	6	5	3	1
1	6	3	9	5	7	8	4	2
5	7	2	8	6	9	4	1	3
3	4	6	7	1	5	2	8	9
8	9	1	4	2	3	6	7	5
4	1	5	6	3	2	7	9	8
9	2	8	1	7	4	3	5	6
6	3	7	5	9	8	1	2	4

4-6

2	9	7	4	6	5	8	1	3
4	8	5	1	9	3	2	7	6
1	6	3	8	2	7	5	9	4
5	4	2	3	7	6	9	8	1
9	7	1	2	8	4	6	3	5
8	3	6	5	1	9	7	4	2
3	1	9	6	5	8	4	2	7
7	5	4	9	3	2	1	6	8
6	2	8	7	4	1	3	5	9

4-7

5	3	7	2	8	9	4	6	1
2	9	6	3	1	4	7	8	5
1	4	8	5	7	6	9	2	3
4	6	1	8	5	2	3	7	9
9	8	5	7	4	3	6	1	2
7	2	3	6	9	1	5	4	8
6	5	4	9	2	8	1	3	7
8	1	9	4	3	7	2	5	6
3	7	2	1	6	5	8	9	4

4-8

5	6	2	4	3	1	8	7	9
8	1	9	7	6	2	5	4	3
4	7	3	9	8	5	2	6	1
2	9	7	8	1	6	4	3	5
1	4	8	5	9	3	6	2	7
3	5	6	2	7	4	9	1	8
9	2	5	3	4	7	1	8	6
6	3	4	1	5	8	7	9	2
7	8	1	6	2	9	3	5	4

49

2	3	6	9	7	5	4	1	8
7	8	5	4	6	1	2	3	9
4	9	1	3	2	8	7	6	5
1	6	8	7	9	4	3	5	2
9	7	3	2	5	6	8	4	1
5	2	4	8	1	3	9	7	6
3	1	7	5	8	9	6	2	4
6	4	9	1	3	2	5	8	7
8	5	2	6	4	7	1	9	3

50

4	6	5	2	9	7	1	8	3
1	8	7	6	5	3	2	4	9
2	3	9	1	8	4	5	7	6
7	2	8	5	1	6	9	3	4
9	4	1	8	3	2	7	6	5
6	5	3	4	7	9	8	1	2
3	1	6	9	2	8	4	5	7
8	7	2	3	4	5	6	9	1
5	9	4	7	6	1	3	2	8

51

5	7	8	6	4	2	9	1	3
9	2	4	1	7	3	6	5	8
6	3	1	9	5	8	4	7	2
3	1	6	8	2	7	5	9	4
4	8	7	3	9	5	2	6	1
2	5	9	4	6	1	8	3	7
8	6	3	2	1	9	7	4	5
7	4	2	5	3	6	1	8	9
1	9	5	7	8	4	3	2	6

52

3	6	1	5	4	8	2	7	9
4	2	5	9	7	3	1	6	8
8	9	7	1	2	6	3	4	5
7	4	6	3	8	1	9	5	2
5	3	9	7	6	2	8	1	4
1	8	2	4	9	5	6	3	7
9	1	4	8	3	7	5	2	6
6	7	3	2	5	9	4	8	1
2	5	8	6	1	4	7	9	3

53

2	7	9	4	6	5	3	1	8
5	3	4	9	1	8	6	7	2
6	1	8	3	7	2	5	4	9
4	6	5	1	2	3	8	9	7
9	8	3	5	4	7	2	6	1
7	2	1	6	8	9	4	5	3
1	5	2	8	9	6	7	3	4
3	9	7	2	5	4	1	8	6
8	4	6	7	3	1	9	2	5

54

5	4	1	2	8	7	6	3	9
9	6	8	1	5	3	7	2	4
2	3	7	9	6	4	5	8	1
8	9	6	5	1	2	3	4	7
7	2	5	4	3	8	9	1	6
3	1	4	7	9	6	8	5	2
6	5	9	8	4	1	2	7	3
1	8	2	3	7	9	4	6	5
4	7	3	6	2	5	1	9	8

55

6	5	3	1	2	8	9	4	7
2	4	1	7	3	9	8	5	6
8	7	9	4	5	6	3	1	2
9	1	7	3	4	5	2	6	8
4	8	5	2	6	7	1	3	9
3	2	6	9	8	1	5	7	4
7	3	4	5	9	2	6	8	1
1	9	8	6	7	3	4	2	5
5	6	2	8	1	4	7	9	3

56

8	9	3	5	4	6	2	7	1
2	5	7	1	9	8	6	3	4
1	6	4	7	2	3	5	9	8
7	3	2	9	6	4	1	8	5
5	1	6	3	8	7	9	4	2
4	8	9	2	5	1	7	6	3
9	2	8	6	3	5	4	1	7
6	4	1	8	7	2	3	5	9
3	7	5	4	1	9	8	2	6

5 / 7

8	9	7	5	6	3	1	4	2
5	4	6	8	1	2	9	3	7
1	3	2	9	4	7	5	8	6
4	2	1	7	8	6	3	5	9
9	8	5	3	2	4	6	7	1
7	6	3	1	9	5	8	2	4
6	5	8	4	7	1	2	9	3
3	1	4	2	5	9	7	6	8
2	7	9	6	3	8	4	1	5

5 / 8

3	9	7	2	4	8	6	5	1
1	6	5	9	3	7	2	8	4
2	4	8	1	6	5	3	9	7
9	5	4	8	7	2	1	6	3
8	1	3	6	9	4	5	7	2
7	2	6	3	5	1	8	4	9
5	3	9	4	1	6	7	2	8
4	7	2	5	8	3	9	1	6
6	8	1	7	2	9	4	3	5

5 / 9

4	9	1	2	5	7	8	3	6
8	3	6	1	4	9	2	5	7
2	7	5	8	3	6	4	9	1
5	1	3	9	7	8	6	2	4
6	8	4	3	1	2	5	7	9
9	2	7	4	6	5	1	8	3
7	5	8	6	9	1	3	4	2
3	6	2	7	8	4	9	1	5
1	4	9	5	2	3	7	6	8

6 / 0

5	6	1	7	4	3	9	8	2
3	7	8	1	2	9	6	4	5
4	9	2	5	8	6	7	1	3
2	8	7	9	3	4	1	5	6
6	4	5	8	1	2	3	7	9
9	1	3	6	5	7	4	2	8
7	2	9	4	6	8	5	3	1
8	5	4	3	9	1	2	6	7
1	3	6	2	7	5	8	9	4

6 / 1

8	4	2	3	7	5	1	6	9
3	5	6	4	1	9	7	2	8
9	7	1	6	8	2	4	3	5
6	3	7	9	4	1	8	5	2
5	8	9	7	2	6	3	1	4
2	1	4	5	3	8	6	9	7
7	2	8	1	9	3	5	4	6
1	9	5	8	6	4	2	7	3
4	6	3	2	5	7	9	8	1

6 / 2

8	9	7	1	4	2	5	3	6
2	4	3	7	5	6	8	1	9
1	5	6	8	9	3	2	4	7
5	6	8	9	2	4	1	7	3
7	2	9	3	8	1	6	5	4
4	3	1	6	7	5	9	8	2
9	7	4	5	6	8	3	2	1
6	1	5	2	3	7	4	9	8
3	8	2	4	1	9	7	6	5

6 / 3

9	4	8	7	2	3	5	1	6
6	7	3	8	5	1	4	9	2
5	1	2	9	6	4	3	7	8
3	8	5	4	9	7	2	6	1
2	6	7	5	1	8	9	3	4
1	9	4	6	3	2	8	5	7
8	3	9	1	4	6	7	2	5
7	5	6	2	8	9	1	4	3
4	2	1	3	7	5	6	8	9

6 / 4

6	9	1	3	8	7	2	5	4
2	5	7	1	9	4	6	3	8
3	8	4	5	2	6	1	9	7
5	1	2	9	7	8	4	6	3
8	3	6	4	5	1	7	2	9
4	7	9	6	3	2	5	8	1
9	2	8	7	4	5	3	1	6
1	4	5	8	6	3	9	7	2
7	6	3	2	1	9	8	4	5

65

6	7	9	1	4	5	8	3	2
1	4	2	8	9	3	6	7	5
8	5	3	2	6	7	1	4	9
2	8	4	5	3	1	7	9	6
7	9	1	4	8	6	2	5	3
5	3	6	7	2	9	4	8	1
9	2	7	3	1	8	5	6	4
3	1	5	6	7	4	9	2	8
4	6	8	9	5	2	3	1	7

66

7	5	3	6	8	4	9	2	1
1	8	2	3	9	7	6	4	5
4	6	9	1	2	5	7	3	8
9	4	7	8	3	1	2	5	6
5	2	6	7	4	9	8	1	3
3	1	8	2	5	6	4	9	7
6	7	4	5	1	2	3	8	9
8	9	5	4	7	3	1	6	2
2	3	1	9	6	8	5	7	4

67

8	4	7	5	1	9	6	2	3
2	5	3	8	7	6	1	4	9
9	6	1	3	4	2	7	8	5
7	9	6	1	3	4	2	5	8
5	2	4	6	8	7	3	9	1
3	1	8	2	9	5	4	6	7
1	7	5	4	6	8	9	3	2
4	8	9	7	2	3	5	1	6
6	3	2	9	5	1	8	7	4

68

1	8	6	7	2	9	3	4	5
5	9	4	3	8	6	7	1	2
7	2	3	5	1	4	9	6	8
8	4	5	1	9	7	2	3	6
9	1	2	4	6	3	5	8	7
6	3	7	8	5	2	1	9	4
4	5	9	6	7	1	8	2	3
2	6	8	9	3	5	4	7	1
3	7	1	2	4	8	6	5	9

69

9	2	8	7	6	1	5	4	3
6	5	7	2	3	4	9	1	8
3	4	1	9	8	5	7	6	2
8	1	9	4	5	6	2	3	7
2	7	3	1	9	8	6	5	4
5	6	4	3	7	2	1	8	9
1	3	2	6	4	9	8	7	5
4	9	5	8	1	7	3	2	6
7	8	6	5	2	3	4	9	1

70

7	6	9	1	8	3	4	2	5
3	1	4	9	5	2	8	6	7
5	8	2	7	6	4	1	9	3
2	5	3	4	9	6	7	1	8
9	4	6	8	1	7	3	5	2
1	7	8	3	2	5	9	4	6
4	2	7	6	3	1	5	8	9
8	3	5	2	4	9	6	7	1
6	9	1	5	7	8	2	3	4

71

2	9	6	7	1	8	5	4	3
1	5	8	6	3	4	2	7	9
3	4	7	5	2	9	6	8	1
7	6	3	2	5	1	4	9	8
4	8	2	9	6	3	7	1	5
5	1	9	8	4	7	3	2	6
6	7	4	1	8	5	9	3	2
8	3	5	4	9	2	1	6	7
9	2	1	3	7	6	8	5	4

72

7	6	9	3	1	2	4	8	5
8	2	5	6	9	4	7	1	3
1	3	4	8	5	7	2	6	9
6	4	2	5	3	1	8	9	7
5	9	7	4	8	6	3	2	1
3	8	1	7	2	9	6	5	4
9	1	3	2	4	8	5	7	6
2	5	6	9	7	3	1	4	8
4	7	8	1	6	5	9	3	2

73

4	8	5	7	6	9	2	1	3
7	3	1	8	5	2	4	6	9
9	6	2	4	1	3	8	7	5
1	9	4	3	7	8	6	5	2
3	5	6	9	2	1	7	8	4
8	2	7	6	4	5	3	9	1
5	7	8	2	9	4	1	3	6
6	4	9	1	3	7	5	2	8
2	1	3	5	8	6	9	4	7

74

7	2	6	9	8	1	4	5	3
5	3	1	7	2	4	9	6	8
4	8	9	6	5	3	1	2	7
1	4	5	8	7	6	2	3	9
2	9	7	1	3	5	8	4	6
8	6	3	2	4	9	7	1	5
6	1	4	5	9	7	3	8	2
3	7	8	4	6	2	5	9	1
9	5	2	3	1	8	6	7	4

75

8	4	9	1	5	7	3	6	2
3	1	6	9	4	2	5	8	7
7	5	2	6	8	3	4	1	9
5	3	4	2	7	8	1	9	6
6	7	1	5	3	9	2	4	8
9	2	8	4	6	1	7	5	3
4	9	5	7	2	6	8	3	1
1	8	7	3	9	5	6	2	4
2	6	3	8	1	4	9	7	5

76

5	3	9	6	4	8	7	1	2
4	2	8	1	7	5	3	6	9
6	7	1	3	9	2	8	5	4
3	8	2	9	6	4	1	7	5
9	1	5	2	8	7	6	4	3
7	6	4	5	1	3	9	2	8
1	5	3	7	2	9	4	8	6
2	4	6	8	3	1	5	9	7
8	9	7	4	5	6	2	3	1

77

7	9	2	1	8	3	5	6	4
1	8	4	7	6	5	3	2	9
6	3	5	9	4	2	8	7	1
5	6	7	2	3	9	4	1	8
9	4	1	5	7	8	2	3	6
3	2	8	6	1	4	7	9	5
4	1	3	8	9	7	6	5	2
2	7	6	4	5	1	9	8	3
8	5	9	3	2	6	1	4	7

78

3	6	5	8	1	4	9	2	7
7	4	8	5	2	9	6	3	1
2	9	1	6	3	7	5	4	8
5	2	7	4	9	8	1	6	3
9	3	4	1	5	6	8	7	2
8	1	6	2	7	3	4	9	5
4	8	3	7	6	5	2	1	9
6	7	2	9	8	1	3	5	4
1	5	9	3	4	2	7	8	6

79

9	7	4	6	2	8	3	1	5
1	8	3	9	7	5	2	4	6
6	5	2	4	3	1	9	7	8
8	2	1	7	4	9	5	6	3
5	3	9	1	6	2	4	8	7
4	6	7	5	8	3	1	9	2
2	9	6	3	1	7	8	5	4
7	1	8	2	5	4	6	3	9
3	4	5	8	9	6	7	2	1

80

6	2	7	3	1	4	8	5	9
3	9	8	2	5	7	1	4	6
4	1	5	6	9	8	2	7	3
8	3	9	4	6	1	5	2	7
5	4	6	9	7	2	3	8	1
2	7	1	8	3	5	9	6	4
1	5	4	7	8	9	6	3	2
7	8	3	1	2	6	4	9	5
9	6	2	5	4	3	7	1	8

8/1

4	1	5	9	8	7	6	2	3
6	3	7	4	1	2	8	9	5
8	9	2	3	5	6	7	1	4
7	8	4	5	9	1	2	3	6
2	6	9	7	4	3	1	5	8
1	5	3	2	6	8	4	7	9
9	4	6	1	7	5	3	8	2
3	7	8	6	2	9	5	4	1
5	2	1	8	3	4	9	6	7

8/2

1	7	3	2	8	9	6	5	4
4	8	2	3	5	6	1	9	7
5	6	9	1	7	4	8	2	3
3	9	4	6	1	2	7	8	5
2	1	7	8	9	5	3	4	6
8	5	6	7	4	3	9	1	2
6	3	1	4	2	8	5	7	9
9	4	8	5	6	7	2	3	1
7	2	5	9	3	1	4	6	8

8/3

9	8	6	1	2	5	7	4	3
1	2	3	7	9	4	6	5	8
5	7	4	6	3	8	1	2	9
8	4	9	3	1	7	5	6	2
2	3	1	4	5	6	8	9	7
7	6	5	2	8	9	3	1	4
6	9	8	5	7	2	4	3	1
3	5	7	9	4	1	2	8	6
4	1	2	8	6	3	9	7	5

8/4

9	8	6	1	4	5	3	2	7
3	1	4	2	7	6	8	5	9
7	2	5	9	3	8	6	1	4
8	3	7	6	1	2	4	9	5
1	5	9	7	8	4	2	6	3
6	4	2	5	9	3	7	8	1
4	9	3	8	6	1	5	7	2
2	7	8	4	5	9	1	3	6
5	6	1	3	2	7	9	4	8

8/5

6	3	4	9	5	2	7	1	8
2	9	7	6	1	8	5	3	4
8	5	1	7	3	4	2	9	6
1	8	6	3	7	5	9	4	2
5	7	2	4	9	6	3	8	1
9	4	3	8	2	1	6	7	5
4	1	9	2	6	7	8	5	3
7	6	8	5	4	3	1	2	9
3	2	5	1	8	9	4	6	7

8/6

3	9	6	7	2	4	1	8	5
2	4	8	9	5	1	3	6	7
5	1	7	6	3	8	4	2	9
6	2	5	4	7	9	8	1	3
1	7	3	8	6	5	2	9	4
4	8	9	3	1	2	5	7	6
9	5	2	1	4	6	7	3	8
7	6	4	2	8	3	9	5	1
8	3	1	5	9	7	6	4	2

8/7

6	9	3	1	4	5	2	7	8
2	5	7	3	9	8	6	1	4
4	1	8	2	6	7	3	9	5
7	2	1	8	5	6	4	3	9
9	3	5	4	2	1	7	8	6
8	6	4	9	7	3	1	5	2
3	4	9	7	8	2	5	6	1
1	8	6	5	3	4	9	2	7
5	7	2	6	1	9	8	4	3

8/8

1	3	6	2	7	8	4	5	9
2	8	5	9	4	6	1	3	7
4	9	7	3	5	1	6	2	8
3	7	4	6	8	9	5	1	2
6	2	9	5	1	4	8	7	3
8	5	1	7	2	3	9	4	6
9	4	3	1	6	7	2	8	5
5	6	8	4	3	2	7	9	1
7	1	2	8	9	5	3	6	4

8/9

4	2	8	7	9	1	6	5	3
6	3	5	8	2	4	1	9	7
1	7	9	6	5	3	8	4	2
3	4	1	2	6	8	5	7	9
9	6	7	3	4	5	2	8	1
5	8	2	9	1	7	3	6	4
7	1	6	5	3	9	4	2	8
2	9	4	1	8	6	7	3	5
8	5	3	4	7	2	9	1	6

9/0

4	1	9	5	6	3	2	7	8
8	6	7	4	1	2	3	9	5
3	2	5	9	7	8	6	4	1
7	3	6	2	8	4	5	1	9
5	9	1	7	3	6	8	2	4
2	8	4	1	5	9	7	3	6
9	7	3	6	4	5	1	8	2
6	4	8	3	2	1	9	5	7
1	5	2	8	9	7	4	6	3

9/1

3	8	5	7	4	1	2	6	9
2	1	6	3	9	8	4	5	7
9	7	4	6	5	2	1	3	8
5	3	9	1	2	6	8	7	4
7	6	2	8	3	4	5	9	1
8	4	1	9	7	5	3	2	6
1	2	7	4	6	3	9	8	5
6	5	8	2	1	9	7	4	3
4	9	3	5	8	7	6	1	2

9/2

9	5	7	4	6	2	8	3	1
6	3	8	9	7	1	2	4	5
1	2	4	8	5	3	9	7	6
2	7	3	5	1	9	4	6	8
4	6	9	3	8	7	1	5	2
8	1	5	6	2	4	3	9	7
3	8	1	7	9	5	6	2	4
7	9	2	1	4	6	5	8	3
5	4	6	2	3	8	7	1	9

9/3

9	2	3	5	1	7	6	4	8
4	5	7	3	6	8	1	2	9
8	6	1	4	2	9	7	5	3
7	9	5	8	3	6	4	1	2
1	3	2	9	4	5	8	7	6
6	4	8	1	7	2	9	3	5
3	8	9	7	5	1	2	6	4
5	1	6	2	8	4	3	9	7
2	7	4	6	9	3	5	8	1

9/4

3	8	1	2	7	5	6	4	9
5	9	2	6	4	8	1	7	3
6	7	4	9	3	1	2	8	5
2	6	5	3	1	7	4	9	8
9	1	8	5	6	4	7	3	2
7	4	3	8	2	9	5	1	6
8	5	7	1	9	2	3	6	4
1	3	9	4	5	6	8	2	7
4	2	6	7	8	3	9	5	1

9/5

1	6	9	5	3	2	4	8	7
3	8	7	9	4	6	5	1	2
5	2	4	8	1	7	9	6	3
7	4	1	6	5	8	3	2	9
8	9	3	7	2	4	1	5	6
2	5	6	1	9	3	7	4	8
4	3	5	2	6	9	8	7	1
9	7	2	4	8	1	6	3	5
6	1	8	3	7	5	2	9	4

9/6

2	4	6	9	1	7	8	3	5
8	5	7	2	6	3	4	9	1
9	1	3	5	4	8	2	7	6
7	8	1	4	3	9	6	5	2
4	2	9	7	5	6	1	8	3
3	6	5	8	2	1	7	4	9
1	9	4	3	8	2	5	6	7
5	3	2	6	7	4	9	1	8
6	7	8	1	9	5	3	2	4

97

7	3	1	2	6	9	4	5	8
9	6	5	1	8	4	2	7	3
2	8	4	7	5	3	1	9	6
8	9	2	4	1	7	6	3	5
5	4	7	6	3	2	8	1	9
6	1	3	8	9	5	7	4	2
1	2	9	3	7	6	5	8	4
3	7	6	5	4	8	9	2	1
4	5	8	9	2	1	3	6	7

98

3	1	4	5	6	2	7	8	9
9	5	8	1	7	3	4	6	2
2	6	7	8	4	9	3	1	5
6	7	3	4	2	8	5	9	1
4	9	2	7	1	5	6	3	8
1	8	5	3	9	6	2	7	4
7	4	6	2	8	1	9	5	3
5	2	1	9	3	7	8	4	6
8	3	9	6	5	4	1	2	7

99

5	3	9	1	7	8	2	4	6
8	7	6	9	4	2	1	5	3
4	2	1	5	3	6	7	8	9
9	5	7	2	1	3	4	6	8
6	8	4	7	9	5	3	2	1
2	1	3	8	6	4	5	9	7
3	6	8	4	5	7	9	1	2
1	4	2	3	8	9	6	7	5
7	9	5	6	2	1	8	3	4

100

5	1	9	7	4	3	8	6	2
8	7	4	5	2	6	9	1	3
3	2	6	9	1	8	7	5	4
6	8	2	3	7	4	5	9	1
1	3	7	8	5	9	4	2	6
9	4	5	1	6	2	3	8	7
4	5	8	6	3	1	2	7	9
2	9	1	4	8	7	6	3	5
7	6	3	2	9	5	1	4	8

101

4	7	9	6	3	5	8	1	2
8	1	5	9	7	2	4	3	6
6	2	3	4	8	1	7	9	5
9	6	2	7	1	4	3	5	8
3	4	1	2	5	8	9	6	7
5	8	7	3	9	6	2	4	1
7	3	8	1	6	9	5	2	4
2	9	6	5	4	7	1	8	3
1	5	4	8	2	3	6	7	9

102

8	3	2	1	5	4	9	6	7
5	9	6	8	2	7	1	4	3
4	1	7	3	9	6	8	5	2
1	7	8	4	3	5	2	9	6
3	6	4	2	1	9	5	7	8
9	2	5	7	6	8	4	3	1
7	5	9	6	8	1	3	2	4
2	4	1	9	7	3	6	8	5
6	8	3	5	4	2	7	1	9

103

3	5	8	1	7	6	4	9	2
4	2	6	9	8	5	3	1	7
9	7	1	2	3	4	8	6	5
5	9	2	4	1	7	6	3	8
1	8	4	5	6	3	2	7	9
7	6	3	8	9	2	5	4	1
2	1	9	3	4	8	7	5	6
8	3	7	6	5	9	1	2	4
6	4	5	7	2	1	9	8	3

104

8	7	9	6	2	1	3	5	4
2	4	1	3	5	7	8	6	9
5	3	6	4	8	9	1	2	7
3	1	4	7	6	5	2	9	8
7	6	8	9	1	2	5	4	3
9	5	2	8	3	4	6	7	1
1	2	7	5	4	3	9	8	6
6	9	3	2	7	8	4	1	5
4	8	5	1	9	6	7	3	2

105

1	6	3	8	4	9	2	5	7
9	5	4	2	3	7	6	1	8
2	7	8	6	5	1	3	9	4
7	4	2	1	6	3	9	8	5
3	9	6	7	8	5	1	4	2
8	1	5	4	9	2	7	3	6
5	2	9	3	7	8	4	6	1
6	3	1	5	2	4	8	7	9
4	8	7	9	1	6	5	2	3

106

3	5	7	4	8	9	1	6	2
1	4	9	7	6	2	5	3	8
8	2	6	3	5	1	9	7	4
9	8	3	6	7	4	2	1	5
7	6	5	1	2	8	4	9	3
2	1	4	5	9	3	7	8	6
6	3	2	9	1	5	8	4	7
5	7	1	8	4	6	3	2	9
4	9	8	2	3	7	6	5	1

107

8	9	4	3	6	5	1	2	7
2	6	1	8	7	4	5	3	9
7	3	5	2	9	1	8	6	4
6	1	9	5	8	3	7	4	2
5	4	2	9	1	7	6	8	3
3	8	7	4	2	6	9	1	5
1	7	3	6	4	9	2	5	8
4	2	6	7	5	8	3	9	1
9	5	8	1	3	2	4	7	6

108

2	5	3	4	6	9	8	1	7
8	7	1	2	5	3	6	4	9
9	4	6	7	8	1	2	5	3
1	8	5	3	9	6	4	7	2
6	2	9	5	4	7	3	8	1
4	3	7	1	2	8	5	9	6
3	6	8	9	1	4	7	2	5
5	1	4	6	7	2	9	3	8
7	9	2	8	3	5	1	6	4

109

1	2	7	4	9	8	6	5	3
4	9	5	7	3	6	1	2	8
3	8	6	2	1	5	9	7	4
2	7	8	3	6	9	5	4	1
9	3	1	5	2	4	8	6	7
6	5	4	8	7	1	3	9	2
8	6	9	1	4	7	2	3	5
5	4	3	9	8	2	7	1	6
7	1	2	6	5	3	4	8	9

110

1	2	7	6	3	4	5	9	8
4	6	5	1	9	8	2	7	3
8	3	9	2	5	7	4	1	6
2	5	4	7	1	6	8	3	9
6	9	8	5	4	3	1	2	7
7	1	3	9	8	2	6	4	5
5	7	2	4	6	9	3	8	1
9	8	6	3	2	1	7	5	4
3	4	1	8	7	5	9	6	2

111

6	5	1	2	7	8	3	4	9
8	7	2	3	4	9	1	5	6
3	9	4	6	5	1	7	8	2
1	6	7	9	8	5	4	2	3
4	2	8	7	1	3	6	9	5
9	3	5	4	2	6	8	1	7
2	1	3	5	6	4	9	7	8
7	4	6	8	9	2	5	3	1
5	8	9	1	3	7	2	6	4

112

6	5	9	8	1	7	4	3	2
2	7	4	3	6	5	9	8	1
3	8	1	4	9	2	7	6	5
4	3	7	1	5	6	8	2	9
5	9	8	7	2	4	6	1	3
1	6	2	9	3	8	5	4	7
7	4	3	5	8	1	2	9	6
9	2	5	6	4	3	1	7	8
8	1	6	2	7	9	3	5	4

113

9	5	2	3	6	7	4	1	8
7	1	6	9	4	8	2	5	3
8	3	4	2	5	1	7	6	9
3	6	8	4	9	2	5	7	1
1	2	7	8	3	5	9	4	6
4	9	5	1	7	6	8	3	2
6	8	9	5	1	4	3	2	7
2	4	1	7	8	3	6	9	5
5	7	3	6	2	9	1	8	4

114

5	1	8	6	7	4	3	9	2
6	4	7	2	3	9	5	1	8
2	9	3	1	8	5	6	7	4
8	3	2	7	4	1	9	5	6
9	7	1	8	5	6	2	4	3
4	5	6	3	9	2	7	8	1
3	2	5	9	1	8	4	6	7
1	6	9	4	2	7	8	3	5
7	8	4	5	6	3	1	2	9

115

4	7	6	9	1	2	5	3	8
3	9	1	5	4	8	2	7	6
8	5	2	3	6	7	9	4	1
5	1	3	6	2	4	7	8	9
7	8	4	1	9	3	6	2	5
2	6	9	8	7	5	4	1	3
1	3	7	2	5	6	8	9	4
6	2	8	4	3	9	1	5	7
9	4	5	7	8	1	3	6	2

116

5	3	8	6	9	2	4	1	7
4	2	1	5	7	8	3	9	6
7	6	9	1	4	3	5	2	8
8	1	2	9	3	5	6	7	4
3	7	4	2	1	6	9	8	5
9	5	6	7	8	4	1	3	2
1	8	3	4	6	7	2	5	9
6	9	5	8	2	1	7	4	3
2	4	7	3	5	9	8	6	1

117

8	3	9	6	2	4	5	7	1
5	4	6	8	7	1	9	3	2
2	7	1	3	5	9	6	8	4
7	8	3	5	4	2	1	6	9
1	9	5	7	3	6	4	2	8
4	6	2	9	1	8	3	5	7
6	2	8	4	9	5	7	1	3
3	1	4	2	6	7	8	9	5
9	5	7	1	8	3	2	4	6

118

3	6	1	8	7	2	5	4	9
7	5	8	6	4	9	1	2	3
2	4	9	5	1	3	8	6	7
5	2	6	1	8	7	9	3	4
8	7	3	9	6	4	2	5	1
1	9	4	3	2	5	7	8	6
9	8	7	4	5	6	3	1	2
4	1	2	7	3	8	6	9	5
6	3	5	2	9	1	4	7	8

119

2	7	8	4	5	9	6	3	1
5	4	1	6	7	3	8	2	9
3	9	6	1	2	8	7	5	4
6	3	5	8	1	7	4	9	2
9	2	4	5	3	6	1	7	8
8	1	7	9	4	2	5	6	3
4	6	2	3	8	5	9	1	7
7	8	9	2	6	1	3	4	5
1	5	3	7	9	4	2	8	6

120

8	6	1	9	3	4	7	5	2
4	9	2	5	1	7	6	8	3
3	7	5	2	6	8	4	1	9
9	5	3	8	7	1	2	6	4
1	4	7	6	2	9	8	3	5
2	8	6	3	4	5	9	7	1
5	1	8	4	9	6	3	2	7
6	2	4	7	5	3	1	9	8
7	3	9	1	8	2	5	4	6

121

6	7	4	1	9	2	8	3	5
2	3	1	8	4	5	6	7	9
8	5	9	7	6	3	2	1	4
3	1	5	6	7	9	4	8	2
4	9	8	5	2	1	3	6	7
7	6	2	3	8	4	5	9	1
1	4	6	9	5	8	7	2	3
5	8	3	2	1	7	9	4	6
9	2	7	4	3	6	1	5	8

122

2	7	8	4	1	3	5	9	6
5	4	6	7	2	9	1	8	3
3	1	9	8	5	6	4	2	7
4	6	7	1	9	5	8	3	2
1	3	2	6	7	8	9	5	4
8	9	5	2	3	4	6	7	1
7	5	3	9	4	1	2	6	8
6	2	1	5	8	7	3	4	9
9	8	4	3	6	2	7	1	5

123

7	5	3	4	6	9	2	8	1
9	6	1	5	8	2	3	4	7
2	4	8	3	7	1	6	5	9
3	7	5	2	4	8	1	9	6
4	9	2	6	1	5	7	3	8
8	1	6	9	3	7	4	2	5
5	2	4	1	9	6	8	7	3
1	8	9	7	2	3	5	6	4
6	3	7	8	5	4	9	1	2

124

1	5	4	3	9	7	2	8	6
9	8	2	1	6	5	4	7	3
6	3	7	8	4	2	1	9	5
8	2	1	4	7	6	5	3	9
7	9	3	2	5	8	6	1	4
4	6	5	9	1	3	7	2	8
3	7	8	6	2	4	9	5	1
5	4	9	7	8	1	3	6	2
2	1	6	5	3	9	8	4	7

125

9	4	1	5	7	2	8	6	3
6	8	2	3	9	1	4	7	5
5	7	3	8	4	6	9	1	2
8	1	4	7	2	3	5	9	6
2	9	6	1	5	4	7	3	8
7	3	5	9	6	8	2	4	1
3	2	7	6	8	9	1	5	4
4	6	9	2	1	5	3	8	7
1	5	8	4	3	7	6	2	9

126

5	8	4	9	3	1	6	7	2
9	6	7	2	5	4	3	8	1
1	2	3	6	8	7	9	4	5
7	9	1	3	4	6	5	2	8
3	5	6	1	2	8	4	9	7
2	4	8	7	9	5	1	3	6
8	1	5	4	7	3	2	6	9
4	7	2	5	6	9	8	1	3
6	3	9	8	1	2	7	5	4

127

1	2	3	6	9	8	7	5	4
7	6	4	1	3	5	2	8	9
9	8	5	7	2	4	6	1	3
5	3	8	2	1	7	9	4	6
2	1	9	4	6	3	5	7	8
4	7	6	5	8	9	1	3	2
3	5	7	9	4	6	8	2	1
8	9	2	3	7	1	4	6	5
6	4	1	8	5	2	3	9	7

128

4	8	2	1	5	3	6	7	9
3	5	6	8	9	7	2	1	4
1	7	9	4	6	2	5	8	3
2	4	1	9	3	8	7	5	6
7	6	8	5	1	4	9	3	2
5	9	3	2	7	6	8	4	1
6	3	4	7	2	5	1	9	8
8	1	5	6	4	9	3	2	7
9	2	7	3	8	1	4	6	5

129

9	5	1	8	7	6	4	2	3
2	7	4	3	9	1	6	8	5
6	8	3	5	2	4	9	1	7
3	6	5	7	8	9	1	4	2
7	9	2	1	4	3	8	5	6
4	1	8	6	5	2	3	7	9
8	2	9	4	3	7	5	6	1
5	3	6	2	1	8	7	9	4
1	4	7	9	6	5	2	3	8

130

9	8	4	1	5	3	7	2	6
3	6	2	9	4	7	1	8	5
7	5	1	8	2	6	4	9	3
5	1	6	2	7	9	3	4	8
8	2	9	6	3	4	5	7	1
4	7	3	5	8	1	2	6	9
1	4	7	3	6	8	9	5	2
2	3	8	7	9	5	6	1	4
6	9	5	4	1	2	8	3	7

131

3	9	2	5	6	7	1	8	4
5	4	6	2	1	8	9	3	7
1	8	7	3	4	9	2	5	6
9	3	1	8	2	4	6	7	5
2	7	8	6	5	1	4	9	3
4	6	5	7	9	3	8	1	2
7	1	4	9	3	2	5	6	8
8	5	9	4	7	6	3	2	1
6	2	3	1	8	5	7	4	9

132

9	5	4	1	3	8	7	6	2
7	8	3	9	6	2	1	5	4
6	2	1	5	7	4	9	8	3
2	1	7	6	9	3	5	4	8
8	9	6	4	5	7	2	3	1
4	3	5	8	2	1	6	7	9
5	4	8	2	1	6	3	9	7
1	7	9	3	4	5	8	2	6
3	6	2	7	8	9	4	1	5

133

7	1	5	8	4	3	9	2	6
2	9	8	6	5	1	7	3	4
4	6	3	7	9	2	5	8	1
1	2	6	5	3	9	8	4	7
5	7	4	1	8	6	3	9	2
3	8	9	4	2	7	1	6	5
8	4	7	3	6	5	2	1	9
6	5	2	9	1	8	4	7	3
9	3	1	2	7	4	6	5	8

134

9	6	3	7	5	2	1	4	8
8	5	2	6	1	4	9	3	7
4	7	1	8	9	3	5	2	6
5	8	9	3	7	1	4	6	2
7	2	4	9	8	6	3	5	1
3	1	6	2	4	5	8	7	9
6	3	8	5	2	9	7	1	4
2	4	7	1	3	8	6	9	5
1	9	5	4	6	7	2	8	3

135

3	5	9	7	4	8	2	6	1
2	7	6	3	1	5	4	8	9
1	8	4	9	6	2	5	7	3
6	2	3	5	8	9	7	1	4
9	4	7	1	3	6	8	5	2
5	1	8	2	7	4	9	3	6
7	6	2	4	5	3	1	9	8
4	3	5	8	9	1	6	2	7
8	9	1	6	2	7	3	4	5

136

4	9	6	7	5	1	8	3	2
5	3	7	9	8	2	4	6	1
1	8	2	6	4	3	7	5	9
9	1	3	4	2	7	5	8	6
6	4	5	3	1	8	9	2	7
7	2	8	5	9	6	3	1	4
2	6	9	8	3	4	1	7	5
8	5	1	2	7	9	6	4	3
3	7	4	1	6	5	2	9	8

137

2	5	4	8	9	1	6	7	3
8	6	7	3	5	2	4	9	1
3	9	1	7	6	4	2	5	8
9	7	3	6	2	5	8	1	4
6	8	2	4	1	7	5	3	9
4	1	5	9	3	8	7	2	6
7	3	8	2	4	9	1	6	5
5	4	6	1	7	3	9	8	2
1	2	9	5	8	6	3	4	7

138

5	8	1	4	7	6	9	2	3
3	7	4	9	5	2	6	8	1
2	9	6	1	8	3	4	7	5
7	2	5	8	3	9	1	4	6
6	1	8	2	4	5	3	9	7
9	4	3	7	6	1	2	5	8
8	3	9	6	2	7	5	1	4
1	6	7	5	9	4	8	3	2
4	5	2	3	1	8	7	6	9

139

4	6	1	7	3	9	2	8	5
5	8	2	6	1	4	3	9	7
7	9	3	2	8	5	4	1	6
1	3	6	9	2	8	7	5	4
2	4	7	5	6	1	9	3	8
9	5	8	4	7	3	1	6	2
3	7	5	8	9	2	6	4	1
8	2	9	1	4	6	5	7	3
6	1	4	3	5	7	8	2	9

140

9	6	5	4	1	2	3	7	8
8	7	3	9	5	6	1	4	2
2	1	4	7	8	3	6	5	9
3	5	6	8	9	4	7	2	1
1	2	7	6	3	5	9	8	4
4	9	8	1	2	7	5	6	3
5	8	9	2	6	1	4	3	7
7	3	2	5	4	9	8	1	6
6	4	1	3	7	8	2	9	5

141

3	1	5	4	6	9	8	7	2
6	9	4	8	2	7	5	1	3
2	8	7	5	1	3	9	4	6
7	4	1	6	9	2	3	5	8
8	2	3	1	7	5	4	6	9
5	6	9	3	4	8	7	2	1
9	7	8	2	5	6	1	3	4
1	5	2	9	3	4	6	8	7
4	3	6	7	8	1	2	9	5

142

9	4	6	1	7	3	2	8	5
3	7	5	6	2	8	1	9	4
8	2	1	4	5	9	6	3	7
4	3	8	9	1	2	7	5	6
1	5	2	3	6	7	8	4	9
6	9	7	8	4	5	3	2	1
5	6	3	2	9	1	4	7	8
2	1	9	7	8	4	5	6	3
7	8	4	5	3	6	9	1	2

143

2	3	7	1	6	9	4	5	8
8	1	9	7	4	5	6	3	2
5	6	4	2	8	3	9	7	1
9	2	5	8	3	6	7	1	4
6	7	1	5	2	4	3	8	9
4	8	3	9	7	1	5	2	6
7	5	8	4	9	2	1	6	3
1	4	6	3	5	8	2	9	7
3	9	2	6	1	7	8	4	5

144

7	1	3	9	4	5	8	2	6
6	9	2	7	1	8	5	4	3
5	4	8	2	3	6	1	9	7
1	8	5	6	9	7	2	3	4
4	3	9	1	5	2	6	7	8
2	7	6	4	8	3	9	5	1
3	5	1	8	2	4	7	6	9
9	6	4	5	7	1	3	8	2
8	2	7	3	6	9	4	1	5

145

3	1	7	5	6	4	2	8	9
6	9	8	2	3	7	4	5	1
2	4	5	1	8	9	7	6	3
9	7	2	8	4	3	6	1	5
1	3	4	9	5	6	8	7	2
5	8	6	7	2	1	9	3	4
8	6	9	4	1	5	3	2	7
7	5	3	6	9	2	1	4	8
4	2	1	3	7	8	5	9	6

146

6	4	2	7	9	3	8	1	5
7	3	9	8	5	1	4	2	6
8	1	5	6	4	2	7	9	3
9	5	4	1	3	6	2	8	7
3	7	6	9	2	8	5	4	1
1	2	8	4	7	5	3	6	9
2	8	3	5	1	9	6	7	4
5	9	7	2	6	4	1	3	8
4	6	1	3	8	7	9	5	2

147

7	8	5	6	9	1	4	3	2
1	3	4	7	8	2	6	5	9
2	6	9	4	3	5	7	8	1
8	4	6	2	1	7	3	9	5
9	5	2	3	6	4	8	1	7
3	7	1	9	5	8	2	6	4
5	9	7	8	2	3	1	4	6
6	2	3	1	4	9	5	7	8
4	1	8	5	7	6	9	2	3

148

5	2	9	8	6	4	7	3	1
4	3	6	1	7	5	2	9	8
8	1	7	2	9	3	5	6	4
9	8	2	6	5	1	3	4	7
1	4	3	7	2	8	9	5	6
6	7	5	3	4	9	1	8	2
2	9	8	4	3	7	6	1	5
7	5	1	9	8	6	4	2	3
3	6	4	5	1	2	8	7	9

149

1	4	8	6	9	5	7	3	2
2	7	6	1	8	3	5	9	4
9	5	3	2	7	4	8	6	1
4	6	9	5	1	7	2	8	3
5	2	1	8	3	6	9	4	7
3	8	7	4	2	9	1	5	6
7	9	4	3	5	2	6	1	8
8	3	5	7	6	1	4	2	9
6	1	2	9	4	8	3	7	5

150

6	2	1	7	5	3	4	8	9
5	8	4	9	1	6	2	7	3
9	7	3	8	2	4	6	5	1
8	1	6	3	9	7	5	4	2
4	3	2	6	8	5	1	9	7
7	5	9	2	4	1	3	6	8
1	6	7	4	3	9	8	2	5
2	4	5	1	7	8	9	3	6
3	9	8	5	6	2	7	1	4

151

5	6	7	1	9	4	2	8	3
4	8	3	7	2	6	1	5	9
1	2	9	5	3	8	7	4	6
2	3	8	4	5	1	6	9	7
6	7	1	2	8	9	5	3	4
9	5	4	3	6	7	8	2	1
3	9	2	6	7	5	4	1	8
7	1	5	8	4	3	9	6	2
8	4	6	9	1	2	3	7	5

152

7	4	1	2	3	8	6	9	5
2	6	5	9	4	7	8	3	1
8	9	3	1	5	6	2	7	4
9	3	2	8	1	4	5	6	7
4	5	8	7	6	3	9	1	2
1	7	6	5	2	9	3	4	8
3	1	4	6	8	5	7	2	9
5	2	7	3	9	1	4	8	6
6	8	9	4	7	2	1	5	3

153

8	3	7	4	6	5	1	2	9
2	9	6	7	1	8	3	5	4
4	1	5	2	3	9	8	7	6
1	4	3	5	2	7	6	9	8
5	6	8	9	4	3	2	1	7
7	2	9	6	8	1	4	3	5
6	5	1	3	7	4	9	8	2
3	7	2	8	9	6	5	4	1
9	8	4	1	5	2	7	6	3

154

4	7	5	6	3	8	2	9	1
6	1	9	2	7	5	4	8	3
2	3	8	1	9	4	6	7	5
9	5	7	8	6	2	1	3	4
3	4	2	5	1	7	8	6	9
8	6	1	9	4	3	5	2	7
7	2	4	3	8	1	9	5	6
5	9	3	4	2	6	7	1	8
1	8	6	7	5	9	3	4	2

155

1	3	7	5	6	8	4	2	9
6	9	5	3	2	4	8	1	7
4	2	8	9	7	1	5	6	3
9	4	2	8	3	5	6	7	1
8	1	3	6	9	7	2	5	4
7	5	6	1	4	2	9	3	8
5	8	4	7	1	6	3	9	2
2	7	9	4	5	3	1	8	6
3	6	1	2	8	9	7	4	5

156

2	1	8	5	3	4	9	7	6
6	7	5	9	1	2	4	3	8
9	3	4	6	8	7	5	1	2
3	4	6	7	9	8	1	2	5
7	2	1	3	6	5	8	9	4
8	5	9	2	4	1	7	6	3
1	9	3	8	5	6	2	4	7
5	6	7	4	2	9	3	8	1
4	8	2	1	7	3	6	5	9

157

2	4	5	1	8	3	9	7	6
9	3	1	6	7	5	4	8	2
8	6	7	9	2	4	1	5	3
6	5	2	7	1	8	3	4	9
1	8	9	4	3	2	7	6	5
3	7	4	5	9	6	2	1	8
5	2	8	3	4	7	6	9	1
4	9	3	8	6	1	5	2	7
7	1	6	2	5	9	8	3	4

158

7	1	4	5	8	9	3	2	6
9	8	2	3	7	6	1	4	5
6	5	3	1	2	4	7	8	9
4	9	8	7	5	1	6	3	2
2	3	5	6	4	8	9	1	7
1	6	7	9	3	2	8	5	4
3	7	1	4	9	5	2	6	8
8	4	9	2	6	3	5	7	1
5	2	6	8	1	7	4	9	3

159

4	7	8	6	1	9	5	2	3
2	3	5	7	4	8	6	1	9
1	6	9	5	2	3	4	8	7
9	8	2	4	6	7	3	5	1
5	4	7	8	3	1	9	6	2
6	1	3	9	5	2	7	4	8
3	5	1	2	9	6	8	7	4
7	9	4	1	8	5	2	3	6
8	2	6	3	7	4	1	9	5

160

4	2	6	8	1	3	7	5	9
8	3	7	5	4	9	1	6	2
5	1	9	6	2	7	4	3	8
2	6	4	1	3	5	8	9	7
3	9	8	4	7	6	2	1	5
1	7	5	2	9	8	3	4	6
9	8	1	3	6	2	5	7	4
7	4	2	9	5	1	6	8	3
6	5	3	7	8	4	9	2	1

161

5	1	7	9	4	6	3	2	8
2	9	8	5	3	1	4	6	7
6	4	3	7	8	2	5	1	9
3	8	4	1	6	9	2	7	5
9	2	1	8	7	5	6	4	3
7	6	5	3	2	4	8	9	1
1	7	6	2	5	8	9	3	4
8	3	2	4	9	7	1	5	6
4	5	9	6	1	3	7	8	2

162

4	9	3	1	5	2	8	7	6
8	2	5	3	6	7	4	9	1
7	6	1	9	8	4	5	3	2
1	5	4	6	2	3	9	8	7
3	7	9	8	1	5	6	2	4
6	8	2	7	4	9	3	1	5
9	4	6	2	7	8	1	5	3
2	1	8	5	3	6	7	4	9
5	3	7	4	9	1	2	6	8

163

8	7	2	5	4	6	3	9	1
4	9	3	7	8	1	6	5	2
6	5	1	2	3	9	4	8	7
9	1	4	6	5	7	2	3	8
2	6	8	9	1	3	7	4	5
7	3	5	8	2	4	1	6	9
1	8	9	4	6	2	5	7	3
3	4	7	1	9	5	8	2	6
5	2	6	3	7	8	9	1	4

164

6	1	2	4	8	7	3	5	9
4	7	5	3	1	9	6	8	2
8	3	9	2	5	6	7	1	4
5	2	4	1	3	8	9	7	6
3	9	7	6	4	5	8	2	1
1	8	6	7	9	2	5	4	3
9	4	1	5	7	3	2	6	8
7	6	3	8	2	4	1	9	5
2	5	8	9	6	1	4	3	7

165

8	7	5	6	2	3	9	4	1
6	2	9	5	4	1	8	3	7
1	4	3	8	7	9	6	2	5
2	5	6	3	9	8	7	1	4
4	9	7	1	6	2	5	8	3
3	8	1	4	5	7	2	9	6
5	6	8	2	3	4	1	7	9
9	1	4	7	8	5	3	6	2
7	3	2	9	1	6	4	5	8

166

6	4	9	2	5	3	1	7	8
2	5	3	1	7	8	6	9	4
7	1	8	9	4	6	2	5	3
5	9	7	6	2	4	3	8	1
3	8	4	7	9	1	5	6	2
1	2	6	3	8	5	7	4	9
9	6	5	4	3	2	8	1	7
8	7	2	5	1	9	4	3	6
4	3	1	8	6	7	9	2	5

167

9	7	1	4	3	5	2	6	8
4	2	8	7	9	6	3	1	5
3	6	5	2	8	1	4	9	7
7	4	2	1	5	3	6	8	9
1	9	3	8	6	4	7	5	2
8	5	6	9	2	7	1	4	3
2	3	4	5	1	8	9	7	6
6	8	7	3	4	9	5	2	1
5	1	9	6	7	2	8	3	4

168

6	3	1	5	2	7	4	9	8
2	7	4	3	9	8	1	6	5
5	9	8	4	1	6	3	7	2
3	5	7	2	8	1	9	4	6
8	1	2	6	4	9	5	3	7
9	4	6	7	5	3	2	8	1
7	8	5	9	3	2	6	1	4
1	2	9	8	6	4	7	5	3
4	6	3	1	7	5	8	2	9

169

9	3	2	1	5	8	6	4	7
8	6	5	7	3	4	1	2	9
1	7	4	9	2	6	5	8	3
4	2	7	3	9	5	8	6	1
6	5	1	2	8	7	3	9	4
3	8	9	4	6	1	7	5	2
7	4	6	5	1	2	9	3	8
2	9	8	6	7	3	4	1	5
5	1	3	8	4	9	2	7	6

170

4	9	3	1	5	2	7	6	8
2	6	5	7	8	9	1	3	4
1	7	8	3	6	4	9	2	5
3	2	4	5	1	8	6	7	9
6	8	7	4	9	3	2	5	1
5	1	9	6	2	7	4	8	3
7	3	6	9	4	5	8	1	2
9	5	2	8	7	1	3	4	6
8	4	1	2	3	6	5	9	7

171

6	1	9	3	7	5	8	2	4
3	2	8	6	1	4	7	9	5
7	4	5	8	9	2	6	1	3
5	8	4	2	3	7	1	6	9
9	6	2	1	5	8	3	4	7
1	3	7	9	4	6	2	5	8
2	5	1	4	8	3	9	7	6
8	7	6	5	2	9	4	3	1
4	9	3	7	6	1	5	8	2

172

8	3	6	9	5	4	7	2	1
5	9	2	1	8	7	6	3	4
1	7	4	3	2	6	5	9	8
3	8	7	5	4	9	2	1	6
2	6	1	7	3	8	9	4	5
9	4	5	2	6	1	3	8	7
4	1	3	6	9	5	8	7	2
7	5	9	8	1	2	4	6	3
6	2	8	4	7	3	1	5	9

173

7	3	1	4	8	9	2	6	5
6	8	2	7	3	5	4	1	9
9	5	4	2	1	6	8	3	7
5	6	3	9	2	1	7	4	8
2	7	9	3	4	8	6	5	1
4	1	8	5	6	7	3	9	2
1	9	6	8	7	3	5	2	4
3	4	7	1	5	2	9	8	6
8	2	5	6	9	4	1	7	3

174

2	1	8	5	7	4	3	6	9
4	9	3	8	1	6	2	5	7
6	7	5	3	2	9	8	4	1
5	8	6	1	3	2	9	7	4
1	4	9	7	6	8	5	2	3
7	3	2	9	4	5	6	1	8
9	2	7	6	8	1	4	3	5
3	5	4	2	9	7	1	8	6
8	6	1	4	5	3	7	9	2

175

4	6	7	5	8	3	9	2	1
1	5	3	6	2	9	7	8	4
8	9	2	4	1	7	6	5	3
2	8	1	9	6	5	3	4	7
5	7	4	2	3	1	8	6	9
6	3	9	8	7	4	5	1	2
9	1	8	7	4	6	2	3	5
3	2	5	1	9	8	4	7	6
7	4	6	3	5	2	1	9	8

176

4	9	3	7	5	2	8	1	6
2	8	5	9	6	1	3	4	7
1	6	7	4	8	3	9	5	2
5	7	9	2	4	6	1	8	3
8	2	1	5	3	9	6	7	4
6	3	4	1	7	8	5	2	9
3	1	2	8	9	4	7	6	5
7	4	6	3	1	5	2	9	8
9	5	8	6	2	7	4	3	1

177

5	1	6	2	9	3	4	8	7
7	9	8	6	1	4	3	5	2
4	2	3	8	7	5	6	9	1
8	6	2	3	4	7	9	1	5
3	5	4	9	8	1	7	2	6
9	7	1	5	2	6	8	4	3
6	4	5	1	3	8	2	7	9
2	3	7	4	5	9	1	6	8
1	8	9	7	6	2	5	3	4

178

7	1	8	6	5	9	3	4	2
6	9	2	3	4	8	1	5	7
4	3	5	2	7	1	6	8	9
9	4	7	5	3	6	2	1	8
3	8	1	7	9	2	5	6	4
2	5	6	1	8	4	7	9	3
1	6	9	4	2	7	8	3	5
8	7	3	9	6	5	4	2	1
5	2	4	8	1	3	9	7	6

179

8	6	4	7	3	2	9	5	1
3	7	5	8	1	9	6	4	2
2	9	1	4	5	6	8	7	3
1	2	3	9	6	7	4	8	5
9	8	6	5	4	3	1	2	7
4	5	7	2	8	1	3	6	9
6	1	2	3	7	4	5	9	8
7	3	8	6	9	5	2	1	4
5	4	9	1	2	8	7	3	6

180

4	9	1	6	7	8	2	3	5
6	8	2	3	9	5	1	7	4
7	5	3	2	4	1	8	9	6
2	6	7	4	3	9	5	8	1
9	3	5	1	8	2	6	4	7
1	4	8	7	5	6	9	2	3
3	2	9	5	6	7	4	1	8
5	1	4	8	2	3	7	6	9
8	7	6	9	1	4	3	5	2

181

7	6	9	4	3	2	5	1	8
2	5	1	7	9	8	4	3	6
3	4	8	6	1	5	7	2	9
5	3	7	9	2	4	8	6	1
4	8	2	3	6	1	9	5	7
9	1	6	8	5	7	3	4	2
1	7	5	2	4	9	6	8	3
8	2	3	5	7	6	1	9	4
6	9	4	1	8	3	2	7	5

182

7	6	4	2	9	8	5	3	1
8	3	5	7	4	1	9	6	2
2	9	1	5	3	6	8	4	7
6	1	2	3	7	9	4	5	8
3	7	9	8	5	4	1	2	6
4	5	8	1	6	2	7	9	3
1	4	6	9	2	7	3	8	5
9	8	3	6	1	5	2	7	4
5	2	7	4	8	3	6	1	9

183

5	2	9	1	6	4	7	3	8
1	4	7	2	3	8	9	5	6
6	3	8	7	9	5	2	4	1
8	6	5	9	7	2	3	1	4
9	1	3	4	5	6	8	2	7
2	7	4	3	8	1	6	9	5
3	9	6	5	4	7	1	8	2
4	8	2	6	1	3	5	7	9
7	5	1	8	2	9	4	6	3

184

9	7	6	4	2	8	5	1	3
8	3	2	7	1	5	6	9	4
1	4	5	6	3	9	2	8	7
3	1	8	5	7	4	9	6	2
5	2	4	3	9	6	8	7	1
7	6	9	1	8	2	4	3	5
4	8	1	2	6	3	7	5	9
6	5	3	9	4	7	1	2	8
2	9	7	8	5	1	3	4	6

185

6	2	5	9	1	4	8	3	7
7	1	3	6	5	8	4	9	2
9	4	8	3	7	2	1	5	6
1	8	2	4	3	9	6	7	5
5	7	4	2	6	1	9	8	3
3	6	9	7	8	5	2	4	1
4	9	7	5	2	6	3	1	8
8	5	6	1	4	3	7	2	9
2	3	1	8	9	7	5	6	4

186

2	8	3	4	5	6	1	9	7
7	6	5	8	1	9	2	4	3
1	4	9	7	2	3	5	8	6
6	3	4	1	8	7	9	5	2
5	9	1	3	4	2	6	7	8
8	2	7	9	6	5	4	3	1
9	1	2	5	7	8	3	6	4
3	7	6	2	9	4	8	1	5
4	5	8	6	3	1	7	2	9

187

6	1	4	2	9	8	3	7	5
2	7	9	1	5	3	8	6	4
3	5	8	4	7	6	2	9	1
5	6	1	7	8	4	9	3	2
9	8	7	3	2	5	4	1	6
4	3	2	6	1	9	7	5	8
7	9	6	8	4	1	5	2	3
1	4	5	9	3	2	6	8	7
8	2	3	5	6	7	1	4	9

188

1	6	2	7	5	4	8	9	3
7	9	5	6	8	3	2	1	4
4	8	3	9	1	2	5	6	7
9	2	6	8	3	7	1	4	5
8	3	4	5	2	1	9	7	6
5	7	1	4	6	9	3	2	8
2	4	9	3	7	8	6	5	1
3	5	7	1	9	6	4	8	2
6	1	8	2	4	5	7	3	9

189

6	1	7	3	4	8	5	9	2
3	4	9	2	5	1	8	7	6
2	8	5	9	7	6	3	4	1
4	5	2	8	3	9	6	1	7
7	3	8	6	1	4	2	5	9
9	6	1	7	2	5	4	8	3
1	7	6	5	8	2	9	3	4
5	2	4	1	9	3	7	6	8
8	9	3	4	6	7	1	2	5

190

8	6	3	7	1	5	2	9	4
4	9	2	8	6	3	5	1	7
7	1	5	9	4	2	3	8	6
2	5	4	3	8	7	9	6	1
1	7	9	5	2	6	8	4	3
6	3	8	4	9	1	7	5	2
9	2	7	1	5	4	6	3	8
5	4	6	2	3	8	1	7	9
3	8	1	6	7	9	4	2	5

191

3	9	2	1	7	4	6	5	8
6	7	8	5	9	3	4	1	2
4	5	1	8	6	2	7	9	3
2	3	4	7	8	5	1	6	9
7	1	6	2	3	9	5	8	4
5	8	9	6	4	1	2	3	7
8	6	3	4	1	7	9	2	5
1	2	7	9	5	8	3	4	6
9	4	5	3	2	6	8	7	1

192

9	2	1	3	6	4	5	7	8
3	4	8	2	7	5	9	1	6
5	7	6	8	1	9	4	3	2
2	5	7	1	4	8	6	9	3
8	1	3	9	2	6	7	5	4
6	9	4	7	5	3	8	2	1
4	8	2	5	9	1	3	6	7
7	3	9	6	8	2	1	4	5
1	6	5	4	3	7	2	8	9

193

7	2	5	4	3	9	6	1	8
9	8	4	6	7	1	5	3	2
1	6	3	5	2	8	7	9	4
5	1	8	3	6	2	9	4	7
4	9	7	8	1	5	2	6	3
2	3	6	7	9	4	8	5	1
3	4	9	2	8	6	1	7	5
6	5	2	1	4	7	3	8	9
8	7	1	9	5	3	4	2	6

194

2	3	1	8	9	6	7	4	5
4	5	7	2	1	3	6	9	8
6	8	9	5	4	7	3	2	1
8	7	5	1	3	9	4	6	2
9	2	4	7	6	5	8	1	3
3	1	6	4	2	8	9	5	7
7	6	3	9	5	1	2	8	4
5	9	2	3	8	4	1	7	6
1	4	8	6	7	2	5	3	9

195

5	2	6	9	1	7	3	8	4
3	9	7	2	4	8	6	1	5
4	8	1	6	3	5	7	9	2
9	3	5	8	6	1	4	2	7
2	6	4	7	5	9	1	3	8
1	7	8	4	2	3	5	6	9
7	4	9	1	8	6	2	5	3
8	1	3	5	7	2	9	4	6
6	5	2	3	9	4	8	7	1

196

8	3	2	4	5	7	1	6	9
5	7	6	3	1	9	2	4	8
4	1	9	6	2	8	5	3	7
2	9	1	8	4	5	6	7	3
7	5	8	2	3	6	4	9	1
6	4	3	7	9	1	8	2	5
9	8	7	5	6	4	3	1	2
1	2	4	9	8	3	7	5	6
3	6	5	1	7	2	9	8	4

197

6	7	9	8	2	3	1	5	4
5	8	3	4	1	9	2	6	7
4	2	1	5	7	6	3	8	9
9	4	8	6	5	1	7	2	3
1	3	6	2	8	7	4	9	5
2	5	7	9	3	4	8	1	6
8	6	5	7	4	2	9	3	1
3	9	4	1	6	8	5	7	2
7	1	2	3	9	5	6	4	8

198

6	4	5	8	7	9	2	1	3
3	1	8	2	4	6	5	9	7
2	9	7	3	5	1	6	8	4
1	8	6	4	3	7	9	5	2
5	2	3	9	1	8	4	7	6
9	7	4	6	2	5	1	3	8
4	3	1	5	8	2	7	6	9
8	5	9	7	6	4	3	2	1
7	6	2	1	9	3	8	4	5

199

1	7	2	4	3	8	5	6	9
5	3	4	6	2	9	7	1	8
9	6	8	5	1	7	4	2	3
8	9	5	3	6	2	1	4	7
2	1	3	8	7	4	6	9	5
7	4	6	1	9	5	8	3	2
3	8	9	7	4	1	2	5	6
6	5	1	2	8	3	9	7	4
4	2	7	9	5	6	3	8	1

200

5	4	2	8	1	3	9	6	7
6	3	9	5	7	4	1	2	8
8	7	1	9	6	2	4	3	5
9	8	4	3	2	5	6	7	1
7	2	5	6	8	1	3	4	9
3	1	6	4	9	7	8	5	2
4	5	8	7	3	9	2	1	6
2	6	3	1	5	8	7	9	4
1	9	7	2	4	6	5	8	3

201

3	5	1	6	9	2	4	8	7
4	9	6	3	8	7	2	5	1
7	8	2	1	4	5	6	9	3
5	3	8	4	6	9	1	7	2
9	1	7	2	5	3	8	4	6
2	6	4	8	7	1	9	3	5
6	2	5	9	3	8	7	1	4
8	4	3	7	1	6	5	2	9
1	7	9	5	2	4	3	6	8

202

2	6	3	8	1	5	9	7	4
1	8	7	2	9	4	6	3	5
5	9	4	6	3	7	2	1	8
7	4	1	5	8	9	3	2	6
9	2	5	4	6	3	1	8	7
6	3	8	1	7	2	4	5	9
8	1	2	7	4	6	5	9	3
4	5	9	3	2	8	7	6	1
3	7	6	9	5	1	8	4	2

203

3	2	1	4	9	7	5	8	6
9	8	6	5	3	1	2	7	4
4	7	5	8	6	2	1	9	3
5	3	7	1	4	6	8	2	9
6	4	9	2	8	5	3	1	7
8	1	2	9	7	3	4	6	5
7	6	8	3	2	4	9	5	1
1	9	3	7	5	8	6	4	2
2	5	4	6	1	9	7	3	8

204

2	4	6	1	3	5	9	7	8
3	7	1	9	8	6	4	5	2
8	9	5	2	7	4	3	6	1
7	1	2	8	9	3	6	4	5
9	3	4	6	5	2	1	8	7
5	6	8	7	4	1	2	3	9
4	8	7	3	2	9	5	1	6
6	2	3	5	1	8	7	9	4
1	5	9	4	6	7	8	2	3

205

7	9	4	3	6	8	2	5	1
1	6	5	2	9	7	4	3	8
2	3	8	5	1	4	9	7	6
9	4	6	7	8	5	3	1	2
5	1	3	6	4	2	7	8	9
8	2	7	1	3	9	5	6	4
6	8	2	4	5	3	1	9	7
4	5	9	8	7	1	6	2	3
3	7	1	9	2	6	8	4	5

206

4	8	1	9	2	7	5	3	6
6	9	2	4	5	3	7	8	1
5	3	7	6	1	8	9	2	4
2	1	4	5	9	6	8	7	3
3	7	5	2	8	4	1	6	9
9	6	8	7	3	1	2	4	5
8	4	3	1	7	9	6	5	2
1	2	6	8	4	5	3	9	7
7	5	9	3	6	2	4	1	8

207

3	2	7	8	1	5	6	4	9
4	6	1	7	3	9	2	5	8
8	5	9	4	6	2	3	7	1
7	3	4	1	9	6	8	2	5
5	1	2	3	8	7	4	9	6
6	9	8	2	5	4	7	1	3
1	7	3	5	4	8	9	6	2
9	4	5	6	2	3	1	8	7
2	8	6	9	7	1	5	3	4

208

9	2	7	8	6	5	3	1	4
1	3	4	2	9	7	8	5	6
6	5	8	3	4	1	9	7	2
2	4	3	5	7	6	1	9	8
8	6	9	1	3	4	7	2	5
7	1	5	9	2	8	6	4	3
4	9	6	7	8	2	5	3	1
5	7	2	6	1	3	4	8	9
3	8	1	4	5	9	2	6	7

209

3	5	8	1	7	9	6	2	4
4	1	6	8	2	3	9	5	7
2	9	7	5	4	6	3	1	8
5	8	3	4	9	2	1	7	6
9	7	1	3	6	5	8	4	2
6	4	2	7	1	8	5	9	3
1	3	4	6	5	7	2	8	9
7	6	9	2	8	1	4	3	5
8	2	5	9	3	4	7	6	1

210

6	1	5	3	7	4	8	2	9
8	7	9	6	5	2	4	1	3
2	3	4	8	9	1	7	6	5
9	6	7	1	8	5	3	4	2
5	8	1	2	4	3	6	9	7
3	4	2	9	6	7	5	8	1
1	2	6	5	3	8	9	7	4
7	5	8	4	1	9	2	3	6
4	9	3	7	2	6	1	5	8

211

5	3	1	4	6	8	7	2	9
9	7	8	5	1	2	6	3	4
2	6	4	7	9	3	5	1	8
3	2	9	8	5	4	1	6	7
1	5	7	9	3	6	4	8	2
4	8	6	2	7	1	3	9	5
8	4	3	6	2	5	9	7	1
6	9	2	1	4	7	8	5	3
7	1	5	3	8	9	2	4	6

212

5	1	2	7	8	4	6	9	3
6	4	9	5	2	3	1	7	8
7	3	8	6	9	1	4	5	2
9	8	7	2	4	5	3	6	1
1	2	4	3	6	9	5	8	7
3	5	6	8	1	7	9	2	4
2	9	5	1	3	8	7	4	6
4	6	1	9	7	2	8	3	5
8	7	3	4	5	6	2	1	9

213

4	8	6	9	2	1	3	5	7
7	9	5	8	6	3	1	2	4
2	1	3	5	7	4	6	9	8
9	4	7	1	8	5	2	3	6
5	2	8	7	3	6	9	4	1
6	3	1	2	4	9	7	8	5
3	5	2	4	1	7	8	6	9
1	6	9	3	5	8	4	7	2
8	7	4	6	9	2	5	1	3

214

9	7	2	5	4	3	1	8	6
3	8	4	7	1	6	5	2	9
5	1	6	8	9	2	7	3	4
6	9	3	1	8	4	2	7	5
4	2	1	6	5	7	8	9	3
8	5	7	3	2	9	6	4	1
1	4	9	2	6	8	3	5	7
7	6	8	9	3	5	4	1	2
2	3	5	4	7	1	9	6	8

215

7	8	4	2	1	6	5	3	9
2	5	9	4	8	3	1	6	7
6	1	3	7	9	5	4	8	2
8	6	5	3	4	7	9	2	1
4	9	2	8	5	1	6	7	3
1	3	7	9	6	2	8	4	5
5	2	8	6	7	9	3	1	4
9	7	6	1	3	4	2	5	8
3	4	1	5	2	8	7	9	6

216

6	3	1	7	4	9	2	8	5
2	5	8	6	3	1	7	9	4
9	4	7	2	5	8	3	1	6
4	8	2	5	7	6	1	3	9
3	1	6	4	9	2	5	7	8
5	7	9	1	8	3	6	4	2
8	2	5	9	1	7	4	6	3
1	6	3	8	2	4	9	5	7
7	9	4	3	6	5	8	2	1

217

9	6	7	1	2	5	4	3	8
4	1	5	8	3	7	2	9	6
8	3	2	6	9	4	5	1	7
6	9	1	2	5	8	3	7	4
7	5	4	9	6	3	8	2	1
2	8	3	7	4	1	6	5	9
5	4	9	3	1	6	7	8	2
3	2	8	4	7	9	1	6	5
1	7	6	5	8	2	9	4	3

218

3	5	8	2	9	4	7	6	1
4	2	7	6	5	1	3	9	8
6	9	1	8	7	3	5	4	2
2	7	9	5	6	8	1	3	4
8	6	4	1	3	9	2	5	7
5	1	3	4	2	7	6	8	9
1	4	5	7	8	6	9	2	3
9	8	6	3	1	2	4	7	5
7	3	2	9	4	5	8	1	6

219

1	9	2	7	4	5	8	3	6
5	4	3	1	8	6	7	9	2
8	6	7	3	9	2	5	1	4
3	5	8	9	2	4	6	7	1
2	1	9	8	6	7	3	4	5
4	7	6	5	1	3	2	8	9
6	3	4	2	7	1	9	5	8
9	2	5	4	3	8	1	6	7
7	8	1	6	5	9	4	2	3

220

8	2	4	5	3	7	9	1	6
7	1	6	2	8	9	3	4	5
3	5	9	4	1	6	8	2	7
5	3	2	1	7	4	6	9	8
1	6	8	3	9	5	2	7	4
9	4	7	6	2	8	5	3	1
2	7	3	8	5	1	4	6	9
4	9	5	7	6	3	1	8	2
6	8	1	9	4	2	7	5	3

221

8	3	4	5	6	1	9	2	7
2	9	7	4	3	8	1	6	5
5	1	6	9	7	2	4	8	3
4	5	2	8	1	3	7	9	6
9	8	1	7	5	6	2	3	4
6	7	3	2	4	9	8	5	1
7	4	8	6	9	5	3	1	2
1	2	5	3	8	7	6	4	9
3	6	9	1	2	4	5	7	8

222

4	9	2	3	8	7	1	5	6
8	5	6	1	2	4	7	3	9
7	3	1	6	9	5	4	8	2
1	7	4	5	3	9	2	6	8
3	2	8	4	1	6	5	9	7
9	6	5	8	7	2	3	1	4
2	4	3	9	6	1	8	7	5
5	1	9	7	4	8	6	2	3
6	8	7	2	5	3	9	4	1

223

3	6	4	5	2	1	8	7	9
8	7	2	6	3	9	4	1	5
5	1	9	7	4	8	6	3	2
1	8	5	4	7	6	2	9	3
9	4	6	2	1	3	5	8	7
7	2	3	9	8	5	1	6	4
4	5	8	3	6	7	9	2	1
6	9	7	1	5	2	3	4	8
2	3	1	8	9	4	7	5	6

224

3	6	7	9	4	8	5	1	2
5	4	9	1	2	6	3	8	7
8	1	2	7	5	3	4	9	6
9	8	5	2	1	4	7	6	3
2	3	1	5	6	7	9	4	8
4	7	6	3	8	9	2	5	1
6	9	8	4	3	2	1	7	5
7	5	3	8	9	1	6	2	4
1	2	4	6	7	5	8	3	9

225

1	6	7	4	8	5	2	9	3
3	5	8	6	2	9	4	7	1
4	9	2	1	3	7	5	8	6
7	4	3	9	5	2	6	1	8
6	8	9	7	1	4	3	2	5
5	2	1	8	6	3	7	4	9
8	3	4	5	7	1	9	6	2
9	1	5	2	4	6	8	3	7
2	7	6	3	9	8	1	5	4

226

2	4	9	7	8	5	6	1	3
5	1	3	9	6	2	4	8	7
8	7	6	3	1	4	9	5	2
7	2	5	6	4	8	3	9	1
3	8	1	5	2	9	7	4	6
6	9	4	1	7	3	5	2	8
9	6	2	4	3	1	8	7	5
4	3	8	2	5	7	1	6	9
1	5	7	8	9	6	2	3	4

227

5	4	7	1	6	9	8	3	2
2	6	9	5	8	3	7	1	4
8	3	1	7	4	2	9	5	6
7	2	8	9	3	6	5	4	1
1	5	3	4	2	7	6	9	8
6	9	4	8	1	5	2	7	3
4	7	2	3	5	8	1	6	9
9	1	6	2	7	4	3	8	5
3	8	5	6	9	1	4	2	7

228

3	5	8	7	6	4	2	9	1
6	7	9	2	1	3	5	8	4
2	4	1	8	9	5	3	6	7
5	9	4	1	3	2	6	7	8
7	2	6	4	5	8	1	3	9
1	8	3	6	7	9	4	2	5
4	1	2	9	8	6	7	5	3
8	6	5	3	4	7	9	1	2
9	3	7	5	2	1	8	4	6

229

7	1	2	3	8	4	5	9	6
5	6	8	7	2	9	4	3	1
4	3	9	1	5	6	8	7	2
2	7	1	8	4	3	6	5	9
9	5	6	2	1	7	3	8	4
3	8	4	6	9	5	1	2	7
1	2	3	9	6	8	7	4	5
6	4	7	5	3	2	9	1	8
8	9	5	4	7	1	2	6	3

230

9	3	5	1	8	2	7	6	4
1	6	7	4	5	9	3	2	8
4	2	8	3	6	7	5	1	9
2	8	6	7	3	1	9	4	5
3	1	4	5	9	8	6	7	2
7	5	9	2	4	6	8	3	1
8	9	1	6	2	3	4	5	7
6	4	2	9	7	5	1	8	3
5	7	3	8	1	4	2	9	6

231

9	6	7	3	2	8	5	4	1
5	1	4	6	7	9	3	2	8
8	2	3	5	4	1	9	7	6
2	4	5	9	6	3	1	8	7
7	9	1	2	8	4	6	5	3
6	3	8	7	1	5	2	9	4
3	5	6	8	9	7	4	1	2
4	8	9	1	3	2	7	6	5
1	7	2	4	5	6	8	3	9

232

9	3	7	1	8	2	5	6	4
8	6	2	7	4	5	3	1	9
1	5	4	3	9	6	8	2	7
4	7	8	6	3	9	1	5	2
6	9	5	4	2	1	7	3	8
3	2	1	8	5	7	4	9	6
7	1	9	5	6	8	2	4	3
5	4	6	2	7	3	9	8	1
2	8	3	9	1	4	6	7	5

233

8	6	2	3	5	7	9	1	4
3	5	1	4	8	9	2	6	7
9	7	4	2	6	1	8	3	5
5	1	7	6	9	4	3	2	8
2	8	6	5	1	3	7	4	9
4	9	3	7	2	8	6	5	1
6	4	5	8	7	2	1	9	3
1	3	8	9	4	6	5	7	2
7	2	9	1	3	5	4	8	6

234

2	5	9	7	6	1	8	4	3
1	4	3	9	2	8	6	7	5
6	7	8	4	3	5	2	1	9
5	2	6	1	7	4	9	3	8
8	9	1	3	5	2	7	6	4
7	3	4	6	8	9	5	2	1
4	1	7	5	9	6	3	8	2
3	8	5	2	4	7	1	9	6
9	6	2	8	1	3	4	5	7

235

4	3	6	9	8	1	7	2	5
1	2	9	3	7	5	8	6	4
5	8	7	2	4	6	3	1	9
3	9	2	6	1	4	5	7	8
8	5	1	7	3	9	6	4	2
7	6	4	5	2	8	9	3	1
9	7	8	4	6	2	1	5	3
6	4	5	1	9	3	2	8	7
2	1	3	8	5	7	4	9	6

236

2	7	9	5	8	4	3	1	6
4	5	3	6	2	1	8	9	7
6	1	8	3	9	7	2	4	5
1	9	6	2	3	5	7	8	4
3	4	2	8	7	9	6	5	1
5	8	7	1	4	6	9	3	2
8	6	5	7	1	3	4	2	9
9	2	1	4	6	8	5	7	3
7	3	4	9	5	2	1	6	8

237

7	5	1	4	3	9	8	2	6
9	6	4	2	1	8	5	7	3
3	2	8	5	7	6	1	9	4
6	3	5	9	4	1	2	8	7
4	8	7	3	5	2	9	6	1
1	9	2	6	8	7	3	4	5
2	4	6	1	9	5	7	3	8
8	1	3	7	2	4	6	5	9
5	7	9	8	6	3	4	1	2

238

9	3	7	6	1	8	5	2	4
6	4	8	9	2	5	1	7	3
1	2	5	3	7	4	6	8	9
8	5	4	2	9	1	7	3	6
2	7	6	8	4	3	9	1	5
3	9	1	5	6	7	8	4	2
5	6	3	7	8	2	4	9	1
7	1	2	4	5	9	3	6	8
4	8	9	1	3	6	2	5	7

239

6	9	2	7	5	1	3	8	4
4	5	7	6	3	8	2	1	9
8	3	1	4	9	2	6	5	7
9	7	3	2	6	5	8	4	1
2	1	6	9	8	4	5	7	3
5	4	8	3	1	7	9	6	2
3	2	4	5	7	6	1	9	8
7	8	5	1	2	9	4	3	6
1	6	9	8	4	3	7	2	5

240

1	3	2	9	7	4	8	6	5
8	7	6	2	5	1	9	4	3
4	5	9	6	8	3	2	1	7
7	9	5	3	1	2	6	8	4
2	6	8	5	4	9	3	7	1
3	1	4	7	6	8	5	9	2
6	4	7	8	2	5	1	3	9
9	2	1	4	3	6	7	5	8
5	8	3	1	9	7	4	2	6

241

9	1	6	7	3	2	8	5	4
4	5	7	9	8	1	6	2	3
3	2	8	5	4	6	7	1	9
1	4	3	6	5	7	9	8	2
7	8	2	4	1	9	5	3	6
6	9	5	8	2	3	1	4	7
5	3	9	2	6	8	4	7	1
8	7	1	3	9	4	2	6	5
2	6	4	1	7	5	3	9	8

242

6	8	2	9	1	3	5	7	4
1	9	3	5	7	4	2	8	6
7	5	4	8	2	6	3	9	1
2	6	1	7	9	8	4	3	5
5	3	8	1	4	2	7	6	9
9	4	7	6	3	5	8	1	2
3	7	5	2	6	1	9	4	8
4	2	6	3	8	9	1	5	7
8	1	9	4	5	7	6	2	3

243

1	7	9	4	6	3	2	8	5
4	3	8	2	5	7	1	6	9
2	5	6	1	9	8	4	3	7
6	1	5	9	8	4	3	7	2
8	9	2	3	7	5	6	1	4
3	4	7	6	2	1	5	9	8
7	8	3	5	4	6	9	2	1
9	6	4	8	1	2	7	5	3
5	2	1	7	3	9	8	4	6

244

9	7	8	3	2	4	5	6	1
1	3	5	9	6	7	8	2	4
2	6	4	1	8	5	9	3	7
6	8	1	2	9	3	4	7	5
4	9	3	5	7	1	2	8	6
5	2	7	8	4	6	3	1	9
8	1	6	4	5	2	7	9	3
7	5	9	6	3	8	1	4	2
3	4	2	7	1	9	6	5	8

245

3	9	7	6	5	1	8	2	4
6	5	4	8	7	2	9	1	3
8	1	2	9	3	4	5	6	7
2	6	1	3	9	7	4	5	8
9	7	8	4	6	5	1	3	2
5	4	3	1	2	8	7	9	6
7	2	9	5	4	6	3	8	1
1	3	6	7	8	9	2	4	5
4	8	5	2	1	3	6	7	9

246

3	8	9	1	5	4	7	6	2
4	7	6	9	3	2	8	5	1
1	2	5	6	8	7	4	9	3
6	1	4	2	9	8	5	3	7
8	9	3	5	7	1	6	2	4
7	5	2	3	4	6	9	1	8
9	3	7	8	1	5	2	4	6
2	4	1	7	6	9	3	8	5
5	6	8	4	2	3	1	7	9

247

8	2	6	1	4	9	3	5	7
3	4	1	7	6	5	8	9	2
7	5	9	3	2	8	1	4	6
5	3	7	2	9	1	6	8	4
1	9	8	4	7	6	5	2	3
4	6	2	8	5	3	9	7	1
2	8	3	9	1	4	7	6	5
6	1	4	5	8	7	2	3	9
9	7	5	6	3	2	4	1	8

248

9	8	5	1	2	7	4	6	3
4	7	1	9	3	6	2	8	5
6	2	3	8	5	4	9	1	7
2	4	6	7	9	5	1	3	8
3	5	7	4	8	1	6	2	9
1	9	8	2	6	3	5	7	4
7	1	2	5	4	8	3	9	6
5	3	9	6	7	2	8	4	1
8	6	4	3	1	9	7	5	2

249

2	5	4	6	7	1	9	8	3
7	3	9	4	2	8	1	5	6
8	6	1	9	5	3	7	2	4
4	8	7	2	3	5	6	9	1
5	2	3	1	9	6	4	7	8
9	1	6	7	8	4	5	3	2
6	7	2	8	1	9	3	4	5
3	4	8	5	6	7	2	1	9
1	9	5	3	4	2	8	6	7

250

5	4	8	3	2	6	7	1	9
1	2	6	4	9	7	3	5	8
9	7	3	8	5	1	2	6	4
7	1	5	9	6	8	4	3	2
6	8	2	1	4	3	5	9	7
4	3	9	5	7	2	1	8	6
2	6	1	7	3	9	8	4	5
8	9	4	2	1	5	6	7	3
3	5	7	6	8	4	9	2	1

251

1	3	7	5	4	2	6	9	8
6	4	2	1	8	9	7	5	3
9	5	8	7	6	3	4	1	2
4	8	5	9	2	6	1	3	7
7	6	3	8	1	4	5	2	9
2	9	1	3	7	5	8	6	4
3	7	9	6	5	8	2	4	1
8	2	6	4	3	1	9	7	5
5	1	4	2	9	7	3	8	6

252

2	9	3	7	5	8	4	6	1
6	8	5	4	9	1	7	2	3
1	4	7	3	6	2	5	9	8
7	1	9	5	2	6	3	8	4
5	6	8	9	3	4	1	7	2
3	2	4	8	1	7	6	5	9
8	7	1	6	4	9	2	3	5
4	5	6	2	8	3	9	1	7
9	3	2	1	7	5	8	4	6

253

4	8	6	9	5	1	3	2	7
3	9	1	6	7	2	5	4	8
5	7	2	4	3	8	1	6	9
1	2	4	8	6	3	9	7	5
6	5	8	2	9	7	4	3	1
7	3	9	1	4	5	2	8	6
2	1	3	7	8	9	6	5	4
8	4	5	3	1	6	7	9	2
9	6	7	5	2	4	8	1	3

254

1	2	8	5	7	3	6	9	4
4	6	9	1	8	2	7	3	5
7	3	5	4	6	9	8	2	1
9	1	6	7	3	5	2	4	8
5	4	7	2	9	8	3	1	6
2	8	3	6	1	4	5	7	9
6	5	4	3	2	1	9	8	7
3	9	1	8	5	7	4	6	2
8	7	2	9	4	6	1	5	3

255

7	4	5	9	2	1	3	8	6
8	1	2	3	5	6	9	7	4
3	6	9	4	8	7	5	2	1
9	5	1	2	6	3	7	4	8
2	7	8	1	9	4	6	5	3
6	3	4	8	7	5	1	9	2
1	2	6	7	4	9	8	3	5
5	8	7	6	3	2	4	1	9
4	9	3	5	1	8	2	6	7

256

4	1	5	2	9	7	8	6	3
2	9	3	8	1	6	4	7	5
8	6	7	5	4	3	2	9	1
6	8	9	1	5	2	3	4	7
3	5	2	9	7	4	1	8	6
7	4	1	3	6	8	9	5	2
9	7	6	4	2	1	5	3	8
1	3	4	6	8	5	7	2	9
5	2	8	7	3	9	6	1	4

257

6	9	4	5	1	3	7	2	8
2	3	7	4	9	8	5	1	6
5	8	1	6	2	7	3	4	9
3	7	5	1	6	9	4	8	2
8	1	9	7	4	2	6	5	3
4	2	6	3	8	5	1	9	7
1	6	2	9	3	4	8	7	5
9	5	3	8	7	1	2	6	4
7	4	8	2	5	6	9	3	1

258

7	3	2	6	5	1	9	4	8
6	4	1	8	3	9	7	2	5
5	9	8	7	2	4	3	6	1
4	7	6	1	9	5	2	8	3
9	1	3	4	8	2	5	7	6
8	2	5	3	7	6	4	1	9
3	6	7	5	4	8	1	9	2
2	8	4	9	1	3	6	5	7
1	5	9	2	6	7	8	3	4

259

9	4	8	6	1	2	3	5	7
3	1	5	8	7	9	6	4	2
6	2	7	5	3	4	9	8	1
7	8	4	1	5	3	2	6	9
1	6	2	4	9	8	7	3	5
5	3	9	2	6	7	4	1	8
2	5	1	7	4	6	8	9	3
8	9	6	3	2	1	5	7	4
4	7	3	9	8	5	1	2	6

260

1	3	6	5	8	9	2	4	7
8	9	2	1	7	4	6	3	5
7	4	5	6	3	2	1	8	9
3	5	8	2	9	1	4	7	6
4	7	9	3	5	6	8	1	2
2	6	1	7	4	8	9	5	3
6	1	7	4	2	3	5	9	8
5	8	4	9	6	7	3	2	1
9	2	3	8	1	5	7	6	4

261

1	7	2	4	3	6	9	8	5
4	8	6	1	5	9	2	3	7
5	9	3	8	7	2	1	6	4
2	1	8	6	9	5	4	7	3
7	4	9	2	8	3	6	5	1
3	6	5	7	1	4	8	9	2
9	2	1	5	6	7	3	4	8
8	3	7	9	4	1	5	2	6
6	5	4	3	2	8	7	1	9

262

5	3	6	1	2	8	9	7	4
4	1	9	6	7	5	3	8	2
8	2	7	3	9	4	1	6	5
9	4	2	5	6	3	7	1	8
6	8	5	7	4	1	2	3	9
3	7	1	2	8	9	5	4	6
2	6	8	9	3	7	4	5	1
1	9	3	4	5	6	8	2	7
7	5	4	8	1	2	6	9	3

263

6	3	9	1	8	2	7	4	5
5	1	7	6	9	4	3	2	8
8	4	2	7	3	5	9	1	6
4	5	3	8	7	1	6	9	2
2	8	1	5	6	9	4	7	3
9	7	6	4	2	3	8	5	1
1	6	8	2	4	7	5	3	9
3	2	4	9	5	6	1	8	7
7	9	5	3	1	8	2	6	4

264

2	8	1	3	4	7	5	9	6
7	9	6	5	1	2	3	8	4
5	3	4	8	9	6	1	2	7
8	7	2	1	6	3	4	5	9
3	1	9	2	5	4	6	7	8
4	6	5	9	7	8	2	3	1
6	5	7	4	2	9	8	1	3
1	4	8	7	3	5	9	6	2
9	2	3	6	8	1	7	4	5

265

1	2	6	4	8	7	3	9	5
4	8	3	6	5	9	1	7	2
5	9	7	1	3	2	6	4	8
6	3	5	8	1	4	7	2	9
7	4	2	5	9	6	8	3	1
8	1	9	2	7	3	5	6	4
2	5	4	3	6	8	9	1	7
3	7	1	9	2	5	4	8	6
9	6	8	7	4	1	2	5	3

266

5	8	4	7	3	9	6	1	2
3	9	7	1	2	6	5	8	4
6	1	2	8	5	4	9	3	7
4	5	3	2	9	8	1	7	6
1	7	6	5	4	3	8	2	9
9	2	8	6	1	7	3	4	5
8	4	9	3	6	2	7	5	1
7	6	5	4	8	1	2	9	3
2	3	1	9	7	5	4	6	8

267

9	1	7	6	8	4	2	3	5
3	6	8	5	7	2	9	1	4
5	2	4	9	1	3	7	8	6
8	4	1	7	3	9	6	5	2
7	3	6	4	2	5	1	9	8
2	9	5	1	6	8	3	4	7
1	5	2	3	4	6	8	7	9
6	7	9	8	5	1	4	2	3
4	8	3	2	9	7	5	6	1

268

5	7	4	8	3	6	2	9	1
6	8	1	9	7	2	3	4	5
2	9	3	4	5	1	7	8	6
3	5	7	6	4	9	1	2	8
1	2	6	5	8	3	4	7	9
8	4	9	2	1	7	6	5	3
9	6	5	1	2	4	8	3	7
4	3	8	7	6	5	9	1	2
7	1	2	3	9	8	5	6	4

269

5	9	1	3	7	2	8	4	6
7	4	6	9	5	8	2	3	1
8	3	2	6	1	4	7	9	5
6	5	9	2	3	7	4	1	8
1	2	4	8	6	9	3	5	7
3	8	7	5	4	1	9	6	2
2	6	5	7	9	3	1	8	4
9	1	8	4	2	6	5	7	3
4	7	3	1	8	5	6	2	9

270

8	5	9	4	2	3	1	6	7
3	4	2	1	6	7	5	9	8
7	1	6	9	8	5	4	2	3
9	2	5	3	4	8	7	1	6
6	8	3	5	7	1	9	4	2
4	7	1	6	9	2	3	8	5
1	3	4	8	5	6	2	7	9
5	6	7	2	1	9	8	3	4
2	9	8	7	3	4	6	5	1

271

5	2	9	6	8	1	4	7	3
7	8	3	2	9	4	5	1	6
1	4	6	3	7	5	2	8	9
4	1	8	9	2	3	7	6	5
6	5	7	1	4	8	3	9	2
3	9	2	5	6	7	8	4	1
9	6	4	7	5	2	1	3	8
8	3	5	4	1	9	6	2	7
2	7	1	8	3	6	9	5	4

272

4	5	7	1	6	3	8	9	2
6	9	1	4	8	2	7	5	3
8	2	3	5	9	7	6	4	1
9	6	8	7	2	5	1	3	4
3	7	2	6	4	1	5	8	9
5	1	4	9	3	8	2	6	7
1	8	9	3	7	6	4	2	5
2	4	5	8	1	9	3	7	6
7	3	6	2	5	4	9	1	8

273

6	8	2	3	7	9	5	4	1
7	5	3	6	1	4	9	8	2
9	1	4	8	2	5	3	7	6
5	9	8	2	4	7	6	1	3
4	2	6	5	3	1	8	9	7
3	7	1	9	6	8	4	2	5
2	6	7	4	8	3	1	5	9
1	4	5	7	9	6	2	3	8
8	3	9	1	5	2	7	6	4

274

3	5	1	6	4	2	7	9	8
7	4	8	3	9	5	6	2	1
9	2	6	7	1	8	4	3	5
1	9	4	2	6	7	5	8	3
6	3	7	8	5	9	2	1	4
2	8	5	1	3	4	9	7	6
5	1	3	9	2	6	8	4	7
4	7	2	5	8	3	1	6	9
8	6	9	4	7	1	3	5	2

275

9	2	4	8	5	6	3	1	7
7	5	3	2	4	1	6	9	8
8	6	1	7	3	9	5	4	2
6	1	7	9	2	8	4	5	3
3	9	8	4	6	5	7	2	1
2	4	5	1	7	3	9	8	6
5	8	2	6	9	7	1	3	4
1	7	9	3	8	4	2	6	5
4	3	6	5	1	2	8	7	9

276

5	7	3	6	1	9	4	8	2
6	1	2	7	4	8	3	5	9
4	8	9	2	5	3	7	1	6
3	2	8	9	7	1	6	4	5
9	4	6	5	3	2	1	7	8
1	5	7	4	8	6	2	9	3
7	3	1	8	6	5	9	2	4
2	6	5	1	9	4	8	3	7
8	9	4	3	2	7	5	6	1

277

9	7	8	6	5	3	4	2	1
2	5	3	4	8	1	7	9	6
1	6	4	7	2	9	5	8	3
5	3	2	8	6	7	1	4	9
7	9	1	5	3	4	2	6	8
4	8	6	9	1	2	3	5	7
8	4	5	3	7	6	9	1	2
6	2	7	1	9	5	8	3	4
3	1	9	2	4	8	6	7	5

278

8	4	1	7	3	9	2	5	6
9	3	5	1	2	6	8	4	7
6	2	7	5	8	4	1	9	3
4	8	2	9	6	7	3	1	5
7	6	3	8	1	5	9	2	4
1	5	9	2	4	3	6	7	8
3	7	6	4	9	1	5	8	2
5	9	8	3	7	2	4	6	1
2	1	4	6	5	8	7	3	9

279

5	2	9	8	1	4	6	7	3
3	4	7	6	5	2	8	9	1
6	1	8	7	9	3	4	5	2
4	8	6	2	7	5	3	1	9
7	3	2	1	4	9	5	6	8
1	9	5	3	8	6	2	4	7
9	5	3	4	2	7	1	8	6
2	7	1	5	6	8	9	3	4
8	6	4	9	3	1	7	2	5

280

2	9	3	8	4	5	7	6	1
8	4	1	6	9	7	3	5	2
6	5	7	2	1	3	4	8	9
7	2	6	4	8	1	9	3	5
9	8	5	7	3	6	1	2	4
1	3	4	5	2	9	6	7	8
3	1	8	9	6	2	5	4	7
4	7	9	3	5	8	2	1	6
5	6	2	1	7	4	8	9	3

281

5	2	6	9	1	8	3	4	7
4	7	8	6	3	2	1	5	9
3	9	1	7	4	5	8	2	6
6	1	4	2	5	7	9	3	8
7	3	2	8	9	4	5	6	1
9	8	5	1	6	3	2	7	4
8	5	7	4	2	9	6	1	3
1	4	3	5	8	6	7	9	2
2	6	9	3	7	1	4	8	5

282

3	2	1	6	5	4	9	8	7
8	5	9	7	2	3	1	6	4
6	7	4	8	1	9	5	2	3
7	9	5	1	6	2	3	4	8
1	8	6	3	4	5	7	9	2
4	3	2	9	8	7	6	5	1
9	1	8	2	7	6	4	3	5
5	6	7	4	3	8	2	1	9
2	4	3	5	9	1	8	7	6

283

9	6	4	5	1	3	8	2	7
8	5	1	6	7	2	3	9	4
3	2	7	9	8	4	6	5	1
5	9	6	3	2	7	1	4	8
4	1	3	8	5	6	2	7	9
2	7	8	1	4	9	5	6	3
1	8	9	4	6	5	7	3	2
7	3	5	2	9	8	4	1	6
6	4	2	7	3	1	9	8	5

284

7	1	5	9	3	8	2	6	4
6	3	8	2	4	5	9	1	7
2	4	9	7	6	1	8	3	5
1	5	3	8	7	6	4	9	2
8	9	6	5	2	4	1	7	3
4	7	2	3	1	9	6	5	8
3	8	1	4	9	7	5	2	6
9	2	4	6	5	3	7	8	1
5	6	7	1	8	2	3	4	9

285

8	2	9	4	1	3	7	5	6
5	1	3	9	7	6	4	2	8
4	6	7	2	5	8	3	9	1
7	9	4	1	6	2	5	8	3
6	5	8	3	9	4	2	1	7
2	3	1	7	8	5	9	6	4
1	4	6	5	3	9	8	7	2
9	7	2	8	4	1	6	3	5
3	8	5	6	2	7	1	4	9

286

3	8	9	4	5	1	6	7	2
1	2	5	9	6	7	4	3	8
6	7	4	3	8	2	5	9	1
8	4	6	7	3	5	1	2	9
5	9	1	2	4	8	3	6	7
2	3	7	6	1	9	8	4	5
4	1	2	8	9	6	7	5	3
9	6	8	5	7	3	2	1	4
7	5	3	1	2	4	9	8	6

287

4	9	5	3	8	2	1	6	7
6	8	2	4	7	1	9	3	5
3	7	1	6	5	9	4	2	8
7	5	3	2	9	8	6	4	1
1	4	6	7	3	5	2	8	9
9	2	8	1	6	4	5	7	3
5	6	9	8	4	7	3	1	2
8	1	4	9	2	3	7	5	6
2	3	7	5	1	6	8	9	4

288

6	9	8	3	4	1	7	5	2
7	4	3	5	8	2	9	6	1
2	1	5	9	7	6	8	3	4
4	7	9	1	6	3	2	8	5
3	5	6	2	9	8	4	1	7
1	8	2	4	5	7	6	9	3
9	6	1	7	3	4	5	2	8
8	3	4	6	2	5	1	7	9
5	2	7	8	1	9	3	4	6

289

2	1	8	7	5	3	6	4	9
7	6	4	2	9	8	3	5	1
3	9	5	6	1	4	7	2	8
6	3	9	1	8	5	4	7	2
5	7	1	9	4	2	8	6	3
4	8	2	3	6	7	9	1	5
8	2	6	4	3	1	5	9	7
1	4	3	5	7	9	2	8	6
9	5	7	8	2	6	1	3	4

290

4	7	5	3	1	9	8	6	2
8	6	3	5	4	2	9	1	7
1	2	9	6	7	8	5	4	3
5	4	1	9	8	3	2	7	6
9	8	2	1	6	7	3	5	4
6	3	7	4	2	5	1	8	9
7	9	8	2	5	6	4	3	1
2	1	6	8	3	4	7	9	5
3	5	4	7	9	1	6	2	8

291

1	5	8	3	2	4	9	7	6
4	6	9	8	1	7	3	2	5
7	2	3	5	6	9	1	8	4
8	7	6	1	5	2	4	9	3
5	3	2	9	4	8	7	6	1
9	1	4	6	7	3	2	5	8
3	4	5	7	9	6	8	1	2
6	8	7	2	3	1	5	4	9
2	9	1	4	8	5	6	3	7

292

5	8	7	3	9	6	1	4	2
3	2	4	8	7	1	9	5	6
1	6	9	2	5	4	8	7	3
4	7	6	5	3	8	2	1	9
2	1	8	9	4	7	6	3	5
9	3	5	1	6	2	4	8	7
8	9	3	6	1	5	7	2	4
7	5	2	4	8	9	3	6	1
6	4	1	7	2	3	5	9	8

293

7	9	6	5	8	3	2	4	1
2	4	3	1	9	7	6	8	5
5	1	8	4	6	2	3	7	9
4	8	2	7	1	6	9	5	3
6	3	5	9	2	8	4	1	7
9	7	1	3	4	5	8	6	2
1	6	7	8	3	9	5	2	4
3	2	4	6	5	1	7	9	8
8	5	9	2	7	4	1	3	6

294

2	1	3	6	5	7	4	9	8
7	8	5	1	9	4	6	2	3
9	4	6	8	3	2	5	1	7
6	2	8	9	7	5	1	3	4
3	7	4	2	8	1	9	5	6
1	5	9	4	6	3	7	8	2
5	9	2	7	4	8	3	6	1
8	6	7	3	1	9	2	4	5
4	3	1	5	2	6	8	7	9

295

1	8	6	3	2	5	9	4	7
2	9	3	6	7	4	5	1	8
7	5	4	9	1	8	6	2	3
3	1	2	8	4	9	7	5	6
8	7	9	5	6	2	4	3	1
6	4	5	7	3	1	8	9	2
4	6	8	2	5	3	1	7	9
9	3	1	4	8	7	2	6	5
5	2	7	1	9	6	3	8	4

296

8	3	1	9	4	6	7	2	5
7	2	6	1	8	5	3	4	9
5	4	9	3	7	2	1	6	8
1	7	2	5	6	8	4	9	3
9	8	4	2	1	3	5	7	6
6	5	3	4	9	7	8	1	2
2	6	7	8	3	1	9	5	4
3	9	5	7	2	4	6	8	1
4	1	8	6	5	9	2	3	7

297

3	2	7	1	8	4	6	9	5
9	1	8	6	2	5	4	3	7
6	5	4	7	3	9	1	2	8
7	3	5	2	9	6	8	1	4
8	9	1	5	4	3	7	6	2
4	6	2	8	1	7	9	5	3
1	8	3	9	7	2	5	4	6
2	7	6	4	5	1	3	8	9
5	4	9	3	6	8	2	7	1

298

8	4	9	1	2	7	3	6	5
1	3	2	6	4	5	8	9	7
5	7	6	8	9	3	4	2	1
2	6	3	7	8	9	5	1	4
7	1	4	5	6	2	9	8	3
9	5	8	4	3	1	6	7	2
3	9	1	2	5	6	7	4	8
4	2	5	9	7	8	1	3	6
6	8	7	3	1	4	2	5	9

299

3	4	7	2	9	8	1	5	6
9	1	6	5	3	7	8	2	4
8	5	2	6	4	1	9	7	3
5	8	3	9	7	4	2	6	1
2	7	4	8	1	6	5	3	9
6	9	1	3	2	5	4	8	7
7	3	9	1	5	2	6	4	8
4	6	5	7	8	9	3	1	2
1	2	8	4	6	3	7	9	5

300

2	7	1	6	9	4	5	8	3
3	5	4	8	1	2	7	9	6
9	6	8	7	3	5	1	2	4
6	3	5	1	4	8	2	7	9
7	8	2	9	6	3	4	5	1
4	1	9	2	5	7	3	6	8
1	9	3	5	7	6	8	4	2
5	2	6	4	8	1	9	3	7
8	4	7	3	2	9	6	1	5